WINDMILLS IN MY OVEN

A BOOK OF DUTCH BAKING

For Henk, Judy and Leon,
with love.

The windmill at Geldermalsen in the Betuwe.

WINDMILLS IN MY OVEN

A BOOK OF DUTCH BAKING

SPIEGEL der BEHOUDE NIS

KOSTERS EERSTE PROEFDRUK

TOT KOSTERS EER EN HAARLEMS ROEM

Gaitri Pagrach-Chandra

PROSPECT BOOKS

2002

First published in Great Britain in 2002 by Prospect Books, Allaleigh House, Blackawton, Totnes, Devon TQ9 7DL.

A catalogue entry for this book is available from the British Library.

The maps drawn by James Stewart.
The decorations on the title page and the first page of each chapter reproduce designs used for the moulds of *speculaas* spice-biscuits described in Chapter Ten, below.

ISBN 1-903018-18-8

Typeset in Times Roman and designed by Tom Jaine.

Printed in Great Britain by the Cromwell Press, Trowbridge.

CONTENTS

List of Recipes

A Guide to Dutch Pronunciation

Dutch has several sounds and combinations peculiar to the language, especially vowels and diphthongs. The following examples are meant as a rough guide and are not necessarily a phonetically accepted transcription. I think that people with a Scottish accent will have a natural aptitude as they use many similar sounds.

a   *aah* at the end of a word, in other positions may also be very short, formed lower in the throat than English *a*.

aa *aah*.

e   *uh* at the end of a word or in an unemphasized syllable; *eh* or *ay* as in English *pay* in other positions, depending on the word.

ee *ay* as in English *pay*.

ei as *i* in English *time*, but starting the sound as *eh*.

eu as in French *peu*.

i   as in English *pit*, or in some positions as *ee* as in English *tea*.

ij this is also often written as *y* with an umlaut, diaeresis or two dots on top. The pronunciation is identical to *ei* except in some regional variants where it is pronounced like English *y*.

ie *ee* as in English *tea*.

o   *oh* at the end of a word, without the usual English diphthong sound, more the flatter sound found in northern regional speech, often *o* as in *on*.

oe *oo* as in English *soon*, but with the flatter regional sound.

u   *eu* as in French *peu* but shorter, in some positions as described below.

uu *ü* as in German *über*. To form it, try to say *ooh* with your lips as far forward as possible.

ui this sound stumps most non-natives as there is nothing to compare it with. Its like trying to say *oy* as English *boy*, but starting with an *eh* sound and ending with *ow* as in *owl*, with your lips protruding all the time. You need really agile lips!

b   as in English, except at the end of a word when it is pronounced as *p*.

ch as in Scottish *loch*.

d   as in English, except at the end of a word when it is pronounced as *t*.

g   as in Scottish *loch*, except in southern Dutch dialect when it can be pronounced almost like English *g*.

j   pronounced like English *y*.

n   a final *n* preceded by an *e* is often silent in popular speech.

r   rolled and can be slightly guttural in the South.

w   almost, but not quite like a *v*. The upper teeth are placed slightly more forward on the lower lip and the touch is very fleeting.

Foreword

I would like to thank the three people who were instrumental in bringing about this book: Clarissa Dickson Wright, who encouraged me to write and did her best to smooth my path; Caroline Davidson, my wise and patient agent, who planted and nurtured the seed; and Tom Jaine, my visionary editor, who made it all happen.

I owe a lot to all those, named and unnamed, who helped me in so many ways, by sharing possessions, knowledge and information as well as allowing me to invade their professional and private lives. I would like to thank the following people very warmly: bakers Henk and Martin van Walderveen, Roel and Hans Schroot, Berry van Voorden, Ard Gerards and van Swieten; Theo and Ans Spil of Bakkerijmuseum De Oude Bakkerij; Antje Scheper, formerly of Bakkerijmuseum Het Warme Land; Anke ten Berge and Ron Strik of the Geldermalsen public library; the staff at Foto Aalders; Miller Onclin of Korenmolen de Bouwing; Aafje of Natuurwinkel de Waarde; Anneke Verploeg; Corry Beverloo; Ellen and Maarten Lau; Jan and Aaf Bronts; Wilma Hoek; Henk Fonteyn; Sjaan Roetman; Ad Visscher; Jan van den Broek; Theo Ruissen; Lenie Scholte; and Ivan Day. And of course my husband Henk, and children Judy and Leon, who were always willing to dash off at a moment's notice in search of yet another speciality.

I am grateful to the Koninklijke Bibliotheek in The Hague for supplying the pictures used on pp. 80 and 83; and to the Bakkerijmuseum De Oude Bakkerij for supplying the old photographs shown on pp. 14, 16, 19, 22, and 26.

I enjoyed researching and writing this book and I hope it will give you some pleasure. Although the recipes are preceded in many cases by a generous amount of historical background, they are certainly not museum pieces. They are, almost without exception, items which are made and eaten in contemporary Holland and I hope you will be tempted to try a few. I have made them as practical as possible and the ingredients can be found with little or no effort. I use easyblend yeast, for instance, not the more temperamental fresh compressed yeast. In similar vein, I have substituted vanilla extract for the vanilla sugar which is more common in Holland. I hope you will bear with me for being so precise and long-winded about the spice mixtures as the balance of ready-mixed Dutch *koek* and *speculaas* spices is not the same as British mixed spice. Note too that all the butter specified is unsalted. I should mention that the amount of liquid prescribed in the bread recipes is approximate: if your flour has a particularly high protein content, as do some North American and Australian brands, you may need to increase the liquid slightly. Happy baking!

HOLLAND

Provinces
(districts in lower case).

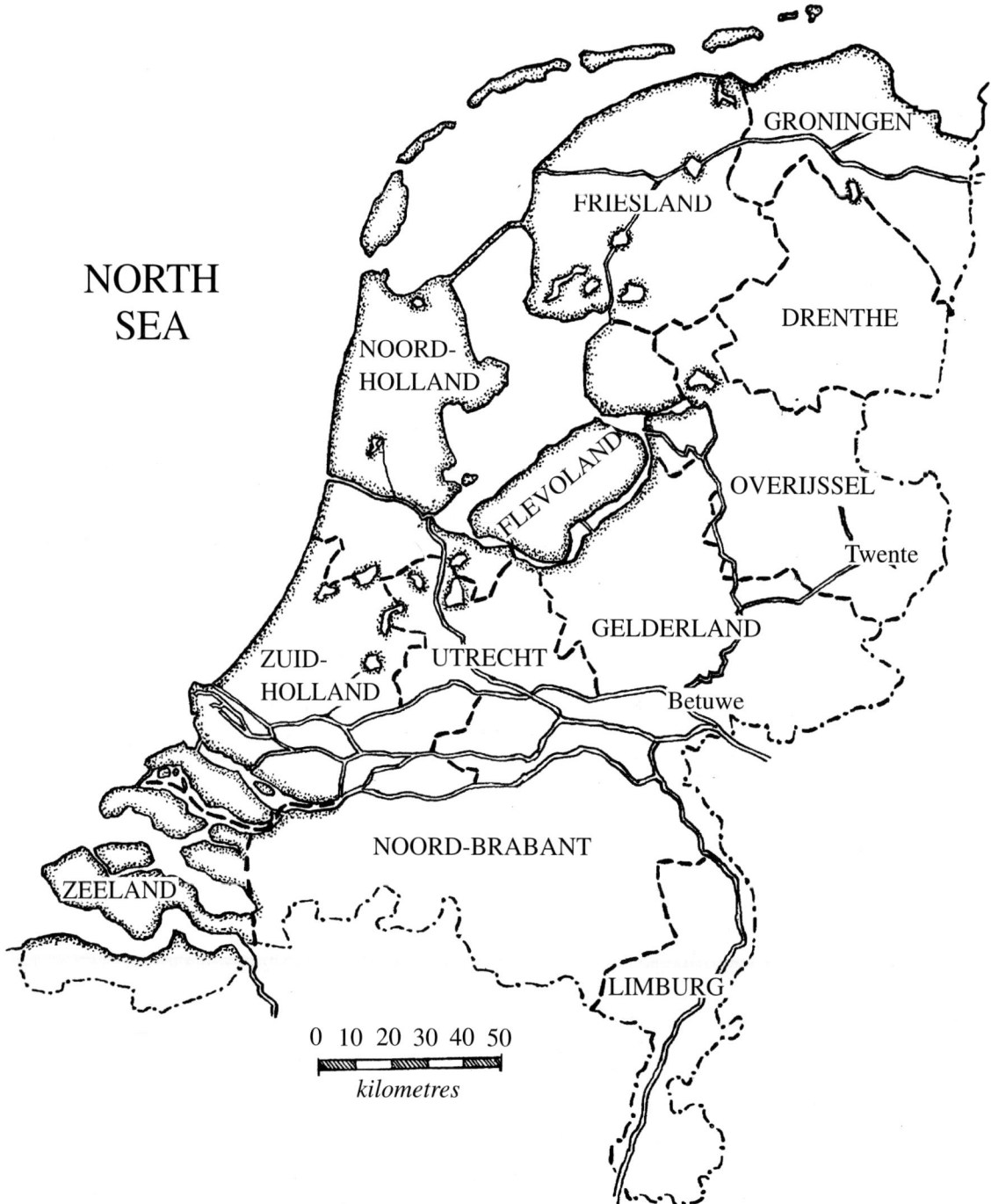

NORTH
SEA

GRONINGEN

FRIESLAND

DRENTHE

NOORD-
HOLLAND

FLEVOLAND

OVERIJSSEL

Twente

GELDERLAND

ZUID-
HOLLAND

UTRECHT

Betuwe

NOORD-BRABANT

ZEELAND

LIMBURG

0 10 20 30 40 50

kilometres

HOLLAND
Places mentioned
in the text.

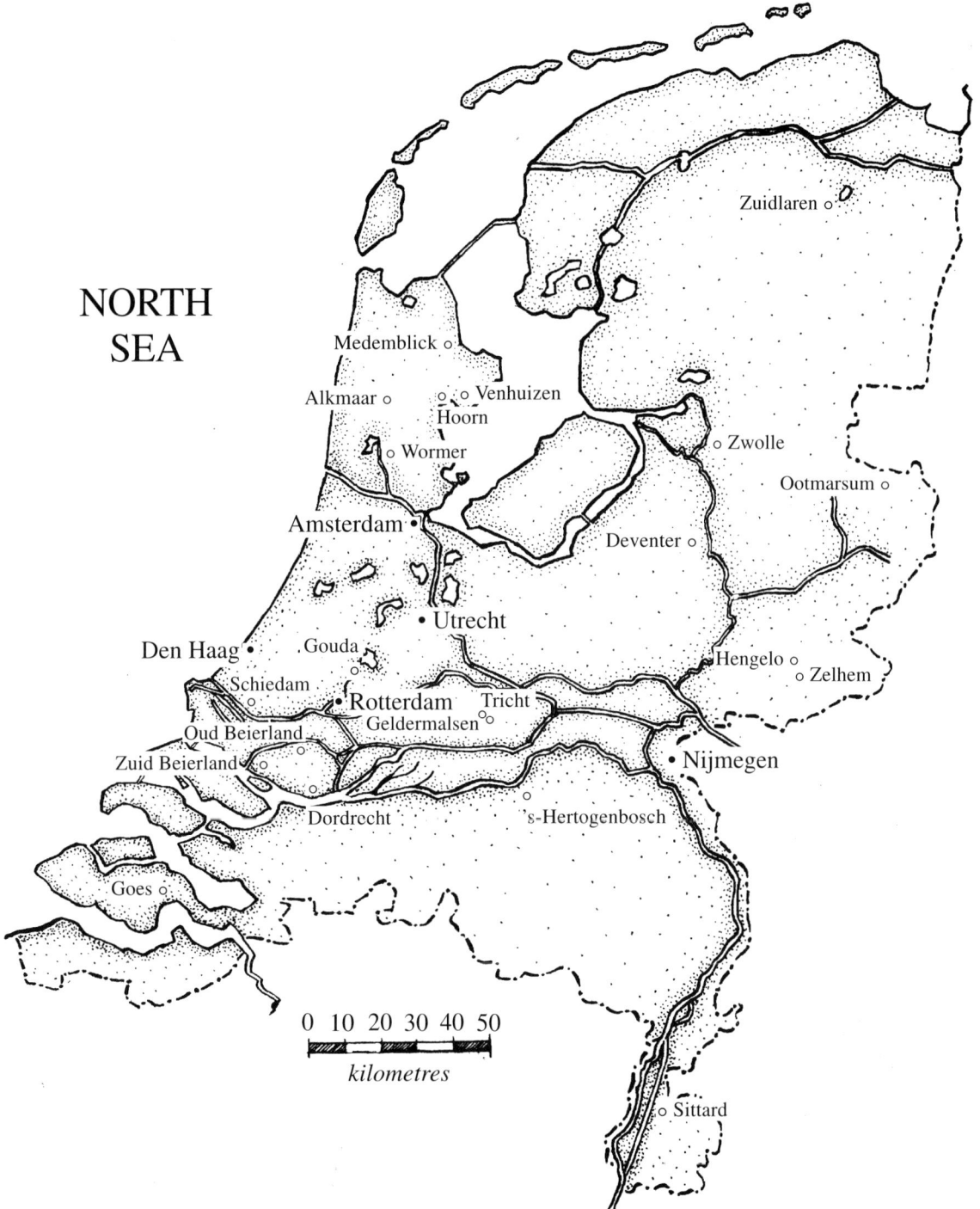

NORTH
SEA

Zuidlaren o

Medemblick o

Alkmaar o   o o Venhuizen
Hoorn

o Wormer

Zwolle o

Ootmarsum o

Amsterdam •

Deventer o

Utrecht •

Den Haag •   . Gouda
o

Schiedam

Hengelo o
o Zelhem

• Rotterdam   Tricht
Geldermalsen o

Oud Beierland

Zuid Beierland o   • Nijmegen

Dordrecht   s-Hertogenbosch

Goes o

0 10 20 30 40 50

kilometres

o Sittard

HOLLAND

Physical features including rivers (named) and canals.

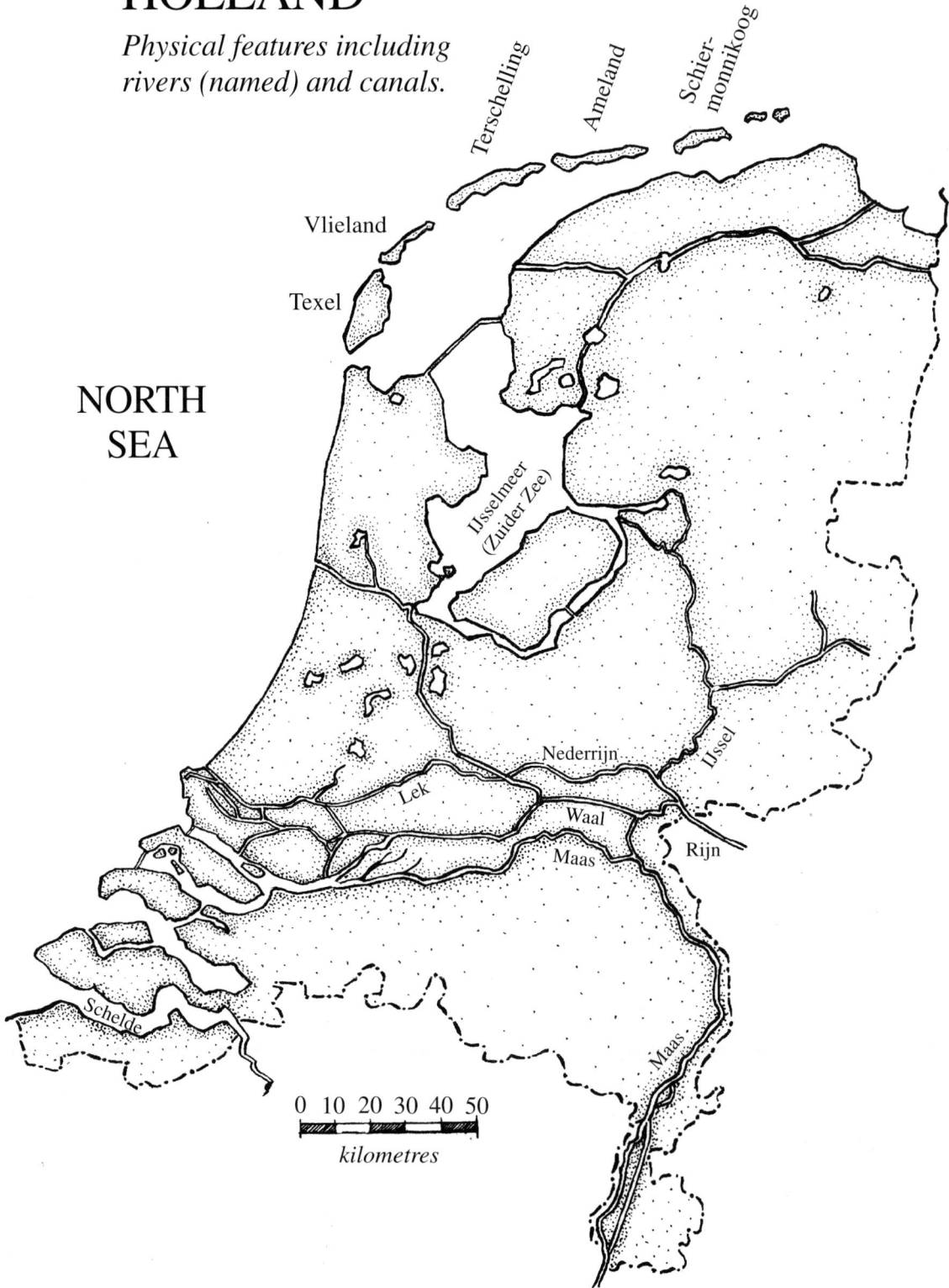

Terschelling

Ameland

Schier-monnikoog

Vlieland

Texel

NORTH SEA

IJsselmeer
(Zuider Zee)

Nederrijn

IJssel

Lek

Waal

Maas

Rijn

Maas

Schelde

0 10 20 30 40 50

kilometres

Chapter One

THE DUTCH BAKER

T his book is about the great Dutch baking tradition, a long and excellent one which has always managed to escape international attention. This is hardly surprising: the Dutch themselves, taking it for granted, often fail to see what is under their noses – a treasure chest of breads, cakes and biscuits, all fascinatingly rooted in social history. It is by no means a dead or even static tradition. Dutch baking is on the move and new trends develop overnight. Good causes, cultural events, world and local politics are all reasons to 'invent' a new bread or cake. Its present breakneck speed makes it all the more important to take stock before panels of this rich tapestry fade beyond recognition.

Large numbers of Dutch people have migrated to all corners of the globe and they have made their mark in international baking, even though it is not always immediately apparent. Not only have they bequeathed the word 'cookie', directly derived from the Dutch *koekje*, to the rest of the world, the English word 'waffle' also has Dutch roots. Some contributions are simply not properly recognized, like the doughnut which is a descendant of the *oliekoek* or *oliebol* taken to America by seventeenth-century settlers. Sometimes the products have developed along their own lines, and seem tenuously bound to the original, or they have paradoxically outlived the original. The South African specialities *vetkoek* and *beskuit* are cases in point. While Dutch *vetkoek* is a kind of fruit pancake, the South African version is a fritter which is split and filled with something sweet or savoury. *Beschuit* is a featherlight yeast rusk while *beskuit* is more like *biscotti*, generally leavened with baking powder and more like the original home-made rusk baked centuries ago in Holland, but which has now ceased to exist in its country of origin. Many of the things which are usually made

Bread deliveries by a variety of methods. From top: a dog-cart; a hand-cart (the baker on the left is the father-in-law of the present curator of the Bakery Museum at Medemblik, the source of these old photographs); a boat, during the great floods of Friesland in 1910 – the bread must get through. The bottom picture is of the mobile baker who calls on our road today.

Overstrooming in Friesland 1910   De broodbakker per Schuit

at home in Holland, like biscuits, pancakes, waffles and fritters, were popularized by Dutch immigrants in the United States and South Africa. Other aspects of the Dutch baking tradition, however, have not travelled so readily, perhaps because bread and cakes were not usually baked at home but by professional bakers. If you routinely bake your own bread you bake it wherever you live. The early settlers, many of them rural families, certainly baked their own loaves, but these have become unrecognizable after so many centuries. The modern immigrant is a product of his time and comes from a bread-buying rather than bread-baking tradition. If you are accustomed to buying your bread you soon learn to like what is available. In a nutshell, the Dutchman is dependent on his baker.

The baker decides what his customers eat. This is one of the reasons that there has been so much regional variety, much of which is unknown outside the area of origin. A speciality can be very local and people in a village a few kilometres away may never have heard of it, let alone tasted it. Many Dutch people seem to view their baker much as a child would a magician or conjurer. They are totally in awe of his ability to produce such a wonderful range of goods ready for them to choose from. It may seem strange, to an outsider, to hear Dutch people just back from an exotic holiday paradise say that the one thing they missed was bread. To an insider, the comment would cause no surprise: a slice of good wholewheat bread with local cheese is a familiar homecoming ritual. They eat the foreign breads, of course, and enjoy them so much that they bring them back: *baguettes*, *croissants*, *ciabatta*, muffins and, paradoxically, doughnuts[1] have become mainstream Dutch bakery items.

Freshly baked bread and simple cakes are readily available in even the smallest of villages. Many have more than one bakery and those without have a daily bread van. Large supermarkets have in-store bakeries and local markets often have more than one bakery stall. This may be great for the consumer but it is proving fatal to the traditional baker. Stiff competition, particularly from supermarkets, has reduced the number of bakeries in Holland by half in the past twenty-five years. City-dwellers are the least faithful to the artisan and one city bakery may serve two to two and a half thousand people. Of course, some of these never actually go to a bakery at all, preferring to pick up their bread on the run in the supermarket. Country people are more willing to walk those few extra metres to buy bread from the 'warm baker', as the baker who bakes from scratch on the premises is called. Consequently, there is still place for a larger proportion of bakers in smaller communities.

Country bakers have always had a special relationship with their customers and are willing to provide whatever services they can. Gone are the days when sliced apples and plump hams, even leafy greens like curly

The first three photographs are from the Bakery Museum in Medemblik. From top: bakers pose in front of a 19th-century oven with batch loaves; an old domestic bread oven, built into the kitchen hearth; a baker and his apprentice, ca. 1927. The bottom picture is of the windmill at Medemblik.

kale,[2] were set to dry in the baker's loft, nor is there any longer a regiment of flour sacks in the bakery, each belonging to a particular customer who specified what kind of bread should be baked from it. But the baker will still sell you a few grams of yeast for your pizza, a kilo or two of flour or any other of his raw materials that takes your fancy, as well as make you a single small diet loaf: salt, gluten or sugar-free or whatever you care to order. He will expect you to pay cash nowadays, but I am quite certain that if you were pressed, or had forgotten your purse at home, he wouldn't refuse you tick. This used to be common practice until well after the middle of the twentieth century.[3] Customers paid weekly or monthly: a social event, accompanied by a drop of something and a pipe or two. Gentleman-farmers sometimes paid annually and their steady custom was so valued that the baker himself might keep clay pipes for their sole use at the pleasant yearly ceremony.[4] While the customer benefitted from credit, officialdom came to take a dim view of it, deeming it unfair competition much in the way the age-old custom of a baker giving customers a festive loaf at Easter and Christmas was seen to be an attempt at bribery.

Baking as a profession tends to run in families. The wife looks after front-of-house while the baker and his largely well-qualified employees do the baking. Sons often

16

follow in the footsteps of their fathers. Daughters seldom become bread bakers as it is so physically demanding, but some learn finer work. A baker is usually well grounded in his trade, training nowadays being varied and flexible: full- or part-time; practical and theoretical; always including an apprenticeship of some kind. After covering the basics, a craft-baker may specialize, taking anything from two to six years at a steady pace before graduation. A bake-off 'baker' in a supermarket, on the other hand, is trained for a week and needs only shove things on trays into the oven – reason enough for bitterness in many a bakery. The clever baker turns it to his advantage and emphasizes the artisanal nature of his work. The stupid one lets himself get caught in price wars which he invariably loses.

As in most of western Europe, the trade first came to notice in the Middle Ages, though only achieved dominance in urban and rural societies in the early modern period.[5] At first, it had been customary for people to bake their own bread, the rich in ovens of their own, the rest in communal ovens. Communal baking became a right in many rural areas and landlords were obliged to provide their tenants with a central oven, a medieval custom which persisted until the eighteenth century in some communities.[6] The privilege turned into a tradition in many cases and communal ovens were still in use in the countryside until the middle of the nineteenth century when professional bakeries gradually started to gain a foothold. Even then, until the early twentieth century, many country people preferred to take their dough to the baker rather than to buy his ready-made loaves.[7]

The baking trade in Holland has been closely regulated since the Middle Ages with strict control over the price, quality and weight. Bakers, of course, protected their own interests, particularly through craft guilds. Understandably, these stood firm against outside competition and one had be a freeman of the city to be a member of its guilds. Applicants had to undergo a rigorous learning and apprenticeship process as well as prove their skill. Bakers didn't always have a separate guild; in some places they joined forces with related trades like millers or brewers. On the other hand, the associations could be very exclusive and rye- and white-bread bakers might belong to separate guilds.[8] The guilds as such were disbanded in the eighteenth century[9] but modern bakers belong to all kinds of professional clubs, co-operatives and organizations. For instance, purchasing-clubs help keep prices significantly under control, members benefit from the bulk-purchasing system, and they rely on them for promotional material and advice.

Originally, the price of bread bore a direct relationship to current grain prices. Local authorities set legal minimum prices as well as maximum.[10] Specially appointed bread-weighers were charged with fixing and proclaiming a weekly price for the various types of bread. Lists were posted in

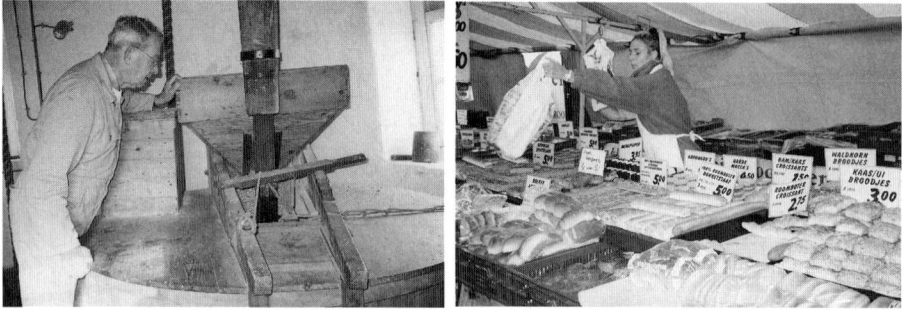

The miller at Geldermalsen feeding grain to millstones revolving in their wooden case (left). The box under his left arm was the receptacle for the customary miller's portion (usually one-sixteenth) levied as fee for grinding the corn. The picture, right, shows a baker's stall at a weekly market.

public places and in bakeries. In the late fifteenth century, in Schiedam just by Rotterdam, the week's prices were announced in church.[11] In theory the bread weighers were supposed to check the quality of the grain but one wonders how this regulation was meant to be interpreted. In Rotterdam in 1703 for instance, three kinds of wheaten bread appear on a weekly list: bread made from best quality Zeeland wheat, bread made from red wheat and bread made from bad wheat.[12] In an ideal situation one could rely on getting what one paid for.

Bakers used their own flour to make loaves to be sold, or they baked the dough brought by customers who were often so mistrustful that they both stamped their initials in the loaf and left someone to oversee the task.[13] These were necessary precautions as adulteration is as old as the baking trade itself. Many bakers proved themselves masters of camouflage. If bean meal was substituted for flour, for instance, chalk might be mixed in to mask the colour change and alum was added to dough to improve the texture.[14] The urge to adulterate generally sprang from pecuniary motives though it was naive idealism that prompted bakers in Arnhem in 1812 to attempt to wipe out part of the French army of occupation by mixing ground glass and copper filings into the dough intended for their bread.[15]

By the mid-fourteenth century it was no longer customary for city dwellers to bake their own bread.[16] Bakers either sold their wares on the premises or at the market.[17] They were obliged to mark their loaves in some way, with a symbol or initials registered at city hall so that fraud could easily be traced to source.[18] In some cities, hawkers bought large quantities of bread to resell door to door. They too were registered; they had to pay dues to the bakers' guilds and were expected to get their bread from one named baker. In other cases, guilds forbade any but the baker himself, his wife, children or servants to deliver bread.[19] As a rule there was no extra charge for delivery, nor is there nowadays, but a survey taken in 1941 showed that a handful of bakers charged a nominal fee for this convenience.[20]

Today, flour comes in sealed sacks, untouched by human hands at any stage of its production. Undoubtedly, the quality is consistent but this has led to an almost boring predictability. The loaves of old were an artisanal product whose quality depended on a harmonious blending of the baker's professional skill and the miller's ability to translate his customer's wishes into reality. The first water-powered mill in Holland is mentioned in documents dating from AD 704, the first windmill from 1274.[21] Windmills remained in use for a long time until they were pushed into the background by modern milling methods developed in the second half of the nineteenth century. Many are still in operation, though most stone-milling (as opposed to industrial steel roller-milling) is done on a small scale. City bakers bought their grain from dealers while their country counterparts got theirs from the farmer.[22] Farmers often took their own grain to be milled and gave the sacks into the baker's keeping, desiring that their bread be baked specifically from that flour. The miller either charged a fee or took a portion of the grain for himself which he could grind and sell. There were, and still are, different millstones suited to the various tasks but grinding rye on the rye-stone and wheat on the wheat-stone was only the beginning; a miller had to be able to combine his knowledge of the grain itself, prevailing climatic conditions and practical mechanics to produce something that would satisfy his customer. And it was largely customized work. Every baker had specific wishes for finer or coarser meal: while one might want his rye crushed very fine, another might want the grains barely broken, yet a third preferred something in between. Millers always had to keep their eyes open. A seventeenth-century household book, *De Verstandige Huys-houdster*, advises moistening the rye before grinding to obtain a light-coloured bread, adding that millers weren't too fond of this practice as they complained it blunted their stones.

The Dirk Slykema bakery in Venhuizen, North-Holland, 1929. The board over the window reads, 'ELECTRIC BREAD, CAKE AND PASTRY BAKERY. THE FUTURE.'

Although grain has been cultivated in Holland for more than six thousand years, the types used for the breads familiar to us can be traced back to the early Middle Ages. Wheat seems to have spread northwards from France in the eighth century AD[23] while rye appears to have come into its own in western Europe in the mid-tenth century.[24] Poor soil, severe winters and lack of moisture, all detrimental to the cultivation of wheat, posed little problem to the hardier rye and, as an added benefit, it ripened earlier than most other grains. Even so, barley and oats were the two most important grain crops in the sixteenth century,[25] providing various forms of sustenance for man and beast. Beer was brewed from barley and both were used in porridges, gruels and breads. Buckwheat is mentioned in the accounts of a Zutphen almshouse in 1390, but it wasn't until the fifteenth and sixteenth centuries that it was cultivated on a significant scale.[26] It was relatively undemanding, though still more difficult than rye. By the second half of the eighteenth century, the popularity of buckwheat had soared, largely owing to the fact that it was not subject to tax.[27] Mixtures of grain were sometimes grown together. *Masteluin*, mentioned as early as 1352, was a mixture of rye and wheat and was used to make a bread of the same name. *Mancksaet* was a mixture of rye and oats, and *spilkoren*, rye and barley.[28]

Due to its vigorous coastwise and maritime trade and to its geographical location – virtually a crossroads of northern Europe – Holland had always had easier access to grain than other European countries. During the famine of 1252 Dutch granaries were full to bursting. This not only helped keep domestic starvation at bay, but large profits were also made by selling to neighbours in need.[29] Grain was imported and exported on a grand scale. By the first half of the seventeenth century, Amsterdam had become the continent's most important grain market.[30] This ready availability of grain contributed to keeping bread prices relatively stable.[31] Foreign competition, coupled to price increases and bad business practices, led to a sharp decline in the domestic grain trade in the eighteenth century,[32] while the ascending popularity of the potato in the nineteenth century dealt another severe blow.[33] This was followed by a growth in the import of cheap American wheat[34] – especially prized for breadmaking as its protein content is higher than most European flours and Dutch flour in particular. Local farmers soon felt the effects and in 1931 the *Tarwewet* (Wheat Law) was introduced, making it compulsory for bread dough to contain a percentage of domestic wheat.

At the same time, increasing industrialization attracted large numbers of people to already well-populated cities. Bread consumption increased exponentially and to meet the growing demand for cheap bread, the first bread factory was set up in 1856 in Amsterdam by the philanthropist Dr Samuel Sarphati. He was concerned that the poor might suffer now that there was no longer price and quality control on bread, and convinced that mechanization would help keep costs down.[35] This factory was followed by a second and a third in 1858 and 1860. By 1870 Utrecht, The Hague, Haarlem and Rotterdam all had their own industrial bakery plants catering for the labouring classes, providing bread at a reasonable price.[36] Bakers responded in two ways. They set up co-operatives which gave customers a proportional refund on what they spent, or the gift of a loaf after a certain number had been bought. Others decided to aim at the top end of the market, producing more luxurious loaves than the run-of-the-mill assortment produced by the factories.[37] While competition was brisk, so was trade. Never before had so much bread been eaten.

The First World War brought about several significant changes, not all of them directly due to war itself but to a combination of circumstances influenced by wartime conditions. Rationing accustomed people to eating less bread than before and they never quite returned to their former voracious consumption. Equally important, working hours improved for many people, including bakers. Abolition of their compulsory night-shifts led to a decline in trade as they could no longer provide enough bread for the early-morning rush. As living conditions improved, people ate less bread and more cooked meals. Many families had lived in very cramped

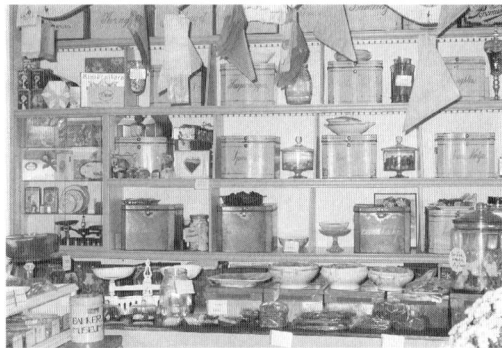

The Bakery Museum at Medemblik has reconstructed this shop interior (top) to accord with the style reigning in about 1900. The large tins were for biscuits, their names lettered on the front. The modern bakery (bottom) is in a village close to my home.

accommodation where there was usually only a single small stove which grudgingly provided warmth and a place to cook one meagre pot of food. As people's means of cooking improved, they turned to more adventurous dishes. The daily norm of three or four bread-based meals had once been commonplace. This pattern was now reduced to two or three in most cases. On the positive side, people could now learn to appreciate the quality of good bread once it was no longer a mere stomach-filler. They could also afford more cakes and biscuits, a craving reinforced by the privations of the Second World War. The fortunate thing is that as prosperity increases so does people's appreciation of good food and this continues to be reflected in Dutch bakery.

An early electric bread van, pictured in front of the Rijksmuseum, Amsterdam. It would hold about 450 loaves and, its manufacturer claimed, could assure the delivery of whole, not broken, biscuits on account of its shock-absorbers.

Chapter Two

BREAD
Brood

Bread has long formed an important part of Dutch people's diets. In the Middle Ages, when it was customary to eat two meals a day,[1] each was composed of bread, with meat or fish for those who could afford it, while the poor had to make do with gruel or porridge. Large slices, or trenchers, of coarse bread would be set on wooden planks or pewter plates before diners[2] and the meat would be served on top of the bread which sopped up all the juices. Finer bread was usually served with the meal in wealthy households and the trencher was often discarded after the meal, given to someone less fortunate. Eating patterns remained virtually unchanged until the seventeenth century, when it became quite common for people to have four meals a day.[3] Except for some rural areas, for example Groningen, where the first two meals relied on root vegetables, bread was generally the basis of all four. The meals themselves were referred to as morning, noon, afternoon and evening *stick, stick* meaning slice of bread.[4] Whether the bread was served plain or not depended on one's means. Breakfast was generally a simple affair, bread with cheese or butter or, if one were wealthy enough, cheese *and* butter.[5] The noon meal was generally the most substantial and, budget permitting, the third course might include sponge cakes and fruit breads, *pofferbroodt*, or other delicacies made of bread like breadcrumbs kneaded with eggs and fried, or slices of bread dipped in egg and fried, or even bread sprinkled with rose-water;[6] light wheaten bread would have been used for such preparations. The mid-afternoon snack, which later became the luxury of tea and sweet cakes and biscuits, was at first just a slice or two of bread with butter or cheese, washed down with cold or warm beer or water.[7] The evening meal varied. It could be as simple as breakfast

or comprise several courses. Porridges were popular, made from rice, oats, barley, millet or a little flour cooked in milk, though the healthiest kind was held to be the *panada* made with breadcrumbs.[8] Even today many people end a main meal with a porridge-like dessert which countryfolk in particular still refer to as porridge.

Three meals a day are usual nowadays and one of these, apart from breakfast, is called a *broodmaaltijd*, 'bread meal'. This has its roots in the nineteenth century and was originally taken in wealthier households. Only later did it become widespread in all layers of society, its aura of luxury fading into something at times quite commonplace.[9] It is a loose term that can apply to a simple sandwich, but it generally means a sit-down meal with a selection of sweet and savoury breads and rolls with various toppings and fillings so that people can put together their own combinations. Sliced bread is usually made into open sandwiches which most people eat with knife and fork. In the seventeenth century the English naturalist and traveller John Ray remarked upon the huge joints of meat dangling from inn rafters in Holland, which were thinly sliced and placed on buttered bread.[10] Such was his obvious distaste at this barbaric practice that one might safely assume that this popular snack, the sandwich, had not yet been inflicted on the British palate.

There has almost always been a 'bread hierarchy'. In the Roman period and Middle Ages the poor ate oatmeal bread or gruel, or barley bread. Barley bread had been the most widely eaten but when rye appeared on the scene in the Middle Ages it was immediately adopted by the wealthy, to be gradually replaced in turn by the more exclusive and expensive wheat. Although barley, rye and wheat were the most important bread grains in the Middle Ages, others were not unknown and oatmeal, buckwheat, millet and rice were used on a smaller scale.[11] In times of scarcity the major grains would be replaced by other things, normally regarded as inferior. In the Middle Ages for instance, peas and beans[12] were ground to make meal and some farmers used chestnuts which rated particularly low on the scale. The surrogates might be used by themselves, or mixed with whichever grain was then in short supply.[13] Later, as eating patterns changed, grains that had previously been significant in the diet were relegated to the status of emergency rations. By the eighteenth century, barley and oats ranked alongside turnips, linseed and beans[14] as a last resort. By the nineteenth century rye and wheat had become the two most important bread grains, which they continue to be.

Coarse pumpernickel-type rye bread similar to the sort eaten today formed an important part of the diet of the more modest and labouring classes from the late Middle Ages onwards. Even so, it was not as cheap as its quality might imply. Between the end of the sixteenth century and the middle of the seventeenth, a skilled artisan or labourer might expect to spend between 17 and 45 per cent of the family income on bread.[15] Such loaves were eventually despised as working-class food. Those who were better situated preferred to eat wheaten bread or very light rye bread made from wheat and rye, referred to as *mistelluyn* in the sixteenth century.[16] By the nineteenth century the term *masteluin* was used to describe the finest type of white bread made with milk.[17]

From the outset, wheaten bread, and white bread in particular, was a luxury. In the Middle Ages there were two general terms current: black bread, referring to coarse rye bread, and white bread referring to wheaten bread. This wheaten bread could be the fine light-coloured bread called 'court bread' or 'gentlemen's bread' or it could be a more common type with fewer of the coarse particles sifted out.[18]

The divide between rye and wheat eating had formed a subtle means of social distinction for a very long time[19] and until the Second World War the consumption of rye bread bore a definite relation to one's income.[20] In the Middle Ages white bread was not something the common man might hope to eat more than a few times during his lifetime – it formed part of the meal of a condemned man in many cities.[21] In 1546 an austerity campaign even forbade white bread made from sifted or bolted flour to be baked in the countryside.[22] Somewhat surprisingly, army rations in 1575 included fine white bread; in 1574 there had only been mention of 'bread',[23] generally used to describe coarse everyday rye bread. By the eighteenth century the difference between country and city bread was well demarcated and rye

Two more bread delivery vehicles from the early part of the last century. The bottom picture is of a contemporary healthfood shop with a good selection of loaves available, although not so wide as would be sold in a specialist bakery.

continued to be preferred in the countryside, with the exception of the western provinces where there was a wheat-growing tradition; this persisted until the Second World War.[24] White bread was eaten by many averagely circumstanced country people on special occasions; for some, this meant only at Easter and Christmas, and sometimes as an accompaniment to special foods like a freshwater perch or strawberries.[25] (Sliced strawberries on white bread continues to be a well-loved treat in modern Holland.) It appears to have been common practice for master and servants to eat bread of differing quality and the 1725 household accounts of a well-to-do family show a larger amount of coarse wheaten bread being bought than the fine white bread which was intended for the family table.[26] In the nineteenth century in Groningen and Friesland, where rye bread was standard, wealthier farmers often ate white bread, but took their meals in a room apart from their staff who had to make do with coarser fare.[27]

White bread had a habit of bringing out peculiarities in people. Country-folk, in particular, allowed themselves to succumb to peer pressure and would go to great lengths to avoid discovery of their occasional purchase of a white loaf. Up to the early twentieth century, many a farmer or house-wife who bought a white loaf for Sunday along with the regular order of rye bread was careful to conceal it from the prying eyes of neighbours.[28] Long before that white bread had been attracting both scorn and envy. In 1641, Pieter van Godewijcx wrote a comedy, *Wittebrootskinderen of Bedorve Jongelingen*, 'White-bread Children or Spoiled Young Things'. Although there is no mention of bread of any kind in the dialogue, the title refers to the spoiled brats of upper-class parents who flaunted their wealth by conspicuous consumption of white bread.[29] Perhaps they were the sort who also used white bread as a cosmetic:[30] mixed with goat's milk and egg-white, it was held to be very effective in lightening the complexion.[31]

In the eighteenth century, at a time when white bread formed a treat, the week following Christmas was referred to by some as *wegweek*, 'fine/white bread week'.[32] The expression 'white bread weeks', *wittebroodsweken*, continues to exist in modern Dutch and means honeymoon, a reminder of another special occasion when one might expect to indulge in fine breads. Many marriage feasts included the *Tulband* described later in this chapter and in some circles a porridge-like confection referred to as *sop* was made for weddings too.[33] For this dish, fine white bread was cooked in milk, often with a few prunes or currants, and served sprinkled with sugar and cinnamon. It was essentially a celebration dish, equally at home on the tables of well-to-do families[34] or on a makeshift trestle outdoors. Until the early twentieth century it was a traditional treat for labourers who had just brought in the harvest.[35]

As one of life's staples, it was fitting that bread was a common form of alms or charity. In many cases, churches issued regular bread tokens to the neediest souls. They might also act for other people, for example, wealthy church-goers who left a bequest for a single almsgiving or, more usually, a yearly one to commemorate the anniversary of their death. Some of these traditions were in continuous existence for several centuries: take the legacy of one Fop Heyniszoon, which lasted from 1468 to 1912.[36] In north-eastern Holland until the 1950s, it was customary in Agelo to hold a Whit Monday rye bread almsgiving for the poor of Ootmarsum, a custom which started before 1672.[37] Its roots lie in the pre-Christian era when peasants from round-about would offer up sacrifices in the fields of young rye to propitiate spirits and deities and so protect the crops from the threat of hail.[38] At some of these village or community ceremonies, donors were obliged to bring loaves of a minimum weight. In the Zelhem/Hengelo area in eastern Gelderland, the loaves were distributed on Ascension Day and each coarse rye loaf had to weigh at least 11 kilos or the donor was fined 30 cents for each 500 grams of underweight. It doesn't appear ever to have been necessary to levy a fine as farmers vied with each other to produce the largest loaf: the upshot was a 140-kilo loaf given just before the First World War.[39]

Bread entered into so many traditional ceremonies and rituals. During the week before Lent in the town of Sittard, close to the German border north of Maastricht, they would fling thousands of crescent-shaped rolls down the Kollenberg hill into the waiting hands of eager youngsters: this is usually taken as symbol of the Biblical loaves and fishes.[40] The Leiden tradition of sharing out white bread and herrings to mark the liberation of the city from the Spanish oppressors on 3 October 1574 has debatable origins. It is extremely dubious whether the ravenous and newly-liberated citizens indeed received white bread and herring to stay their hunger. The first commemoration was in 1774 and the actual custom of giving bread and herring to the poor appears to date from 1823.[41] Until quite recently, *Wieringer tulen* were baked in July for the Wieringen fair.[42] These delicate white rolls, with or without dried fruit, were traditionally distributed on the last Thursday of the month. Local custom dictated that tenant farmers paid their rent on that day to the landowning family from the island of Texel. Business concluded, the rolls would be offered. After 1893, there was no longer any need to pay rent in this way but the custom persisted and the *tulen* continued to go hand in hand with the fair.[43] And there was a special way to eat them: the bottom was cut off the warm rolls and a knob of butter inserted into the crumb. When the butter had melted, the soft part of the roll was extracted with the fingers and eaten, then the remaining shell was buttered and eaten with ham.[44]

Generations of doctors have mused and opined on bread. The great German scholastic philosopher Albertus Magnus speculated on whether wheaten bread was better than barley bread.[45] In the first half of the seventeenth century, Johan van Beverwijck considered, as Galen had before him, that fine wheat bread was the best, followed by wheat bread with the coarsest particles removed, then bread made from the whole grain – with bread made from little more than the chaff and coarse remnants which had been sifted out from finer flour bringing up in the rear, particularly suspect because of its laxative effect.[46] In 1683, the Amsterdam practitioner Stephanus Blankaart produced a New Year's gift for his patients: a 192-page book crammed with advice on what to eat and what to avoid.[47] Many of his ideas (though not always his justifications) were not incompatible with modern nutritional principles. He stressed the health-giving properties of the rougher types, deeming coarse rye bread particularly suitable for those involved in hard physical labour. White bread caused constipation and was also the cause of the deathly pallor of the *wittebroodskinderen* mentioned earlier, giving them worms and unhealthily hard stomachs. He also believed that yeast or sourdough leaven made bread more easily digestible.[48]

Yeast was the leaven of preference in Dutch breads, and recipes in manuscripts and cookery books dating from the late Middle Ages frequently employ *ghest* or *gest* as a raising agent. Regulations in Utrecht dating from 1341 stipulated in most cases that the loaves be leavened with yeast.[49] In 1538, the Zierikzee physician Jason van Praet listed the properties of the three main types of bread. That made from whole grain, mixed with a little yeast, was good for fat people and those with small stomachs. Brown bread with the coarsest particles removed, baked with slightly more yeast, was good for healthy people, an opinion echoed by Doctor Ludeman in 1760. Fine white bread, baked with a generous amount of yeast, properly kneaded and proofed, was ideal for weakened, thin people and those who needed extra nutrition. Bread without yeast, he stressed, was not good for anyone.[50]

Yeast would have been used in its most primitive form, the natural yeast that rose to the surface of beer and spirits, or the dregs left in kegs, and could not be relied upon to give consistent results. A nineteenth-century cookery book[51] gives the housewife advice on how best to keep this kind of yeast, methods which had probably been used for centuries. The author points out quite logically that ridding the yeast of acidic impurities by washing will obviously enhance its keeping qualities. It can then be stored in a jar covered with a piece of bladder pricked with a needle to allow any gas to escape. Liquid yeast may also be put in a well-sealed jar which is then suspended in a well or buried under sand in a cool cellar. Pouring olive oil over the surface of the yeast appears to lengthen its shelf-life. If washed yeast is mixed with enough sugar to form a thin syrup it will keep even better. If the yeast is to be kept for a really long time, it has to be dried. The yeast is washed and laid on a cloth or absorbent paper. Once the water has run off, it can be dried in an oven (which sounds rather risky) or in the open air.

Dutch distillers had been experimenting with yeast for years and around 1780 they developed a marketable paste. This was further refined by a German yeast-maker who produced the first commercial cakes of compressed yeast in 1825. But Dutch bakers and distillers still strove for perfection and offered a premium for the best yeast. The reward went to a Viennese distiller who produced a yeast from grain-must which was used in Europe until 1914.[52] A Dutch chemist, his enthusiasm fired by the the new type of yeast, went to Vienna to learn the process and a few years later he set up a factory in Holland. Holland soon started exporting yeast and, at the beginning, most of the commercial yeast used in the United Kingdom came from Holland.[53] Today Holland is one of the world's leading yeast manufacturers, producing not only for the domestic market but making customized versions for bakers in several other countries.

Loaf shapes

Bread tins have been in common use since the nineteenth century.[54] Before that, loaves were baked on the oven floor and, as the ovens of old were habitually fed with wood and twigs, the loaves had a characteristic taste and texture. In addition, no improvers of the types so favoured today by com mercial bakers were used and the crumb was more compact than modern tastes dictate. These old-fashioned loaves are no longer matter of course but wholefood shops and specialist bakers still provide something similar. Rye loaves were usually rectangular; those made from finer flour were often round and rolls were baked individually or in clusters of six or eight which could later be pulled apart.[55] The latter type is still made today, though the clusters have increased in size coming, as they often do, from a production line. This bland and woolly roll has often been criticized, and justly so. Fortunately, there are still many bakers who bake smaller batches of really tasty rolls – at a price.

Some loaf-shapes and types have faded into obscurity. The Amsterdam or French *knipbrood* is no longer well known, nor is the Rotterdam *scheurbrood*, 'tear bread'. The first was similar to the *knipbrood* described below, save that it was not baked in a tin and a special scissor tool was used to make multiple parallel cuts, resulting in a wide, flattish loaf with a great expanse of crust. The Rotterdam loaf was shaped in a peculiar way: a flattened piece of dough was rolled from both ends towards the centre and the middle of the baked loaf 'tore' itself open: hence its name. In the university town of Leiden, the *Leidse hoogjes* (Leiden 'high ones') were popular with the students, the size being just right for a single person. Tall strips of dough were pressed against each other on the sheet, making individual, high tear-apart loaves, rather like if you slice a large loaf three or four times over its entire length.[56]

Nowadays basic loaves can be divided into three main categories, *plaatbrood* (sheet or batch bread), *vloerbrood* (floor or hearth bread) and *busbrood* (pan bread). Batch bread is baked on a large sheet and the finished loaves bake into each other so that they have no side crust when they are separated. Floor bread is baked directly on the oven floor and, depending on the type of oven, the crust can vary from soft to crisp or chewy. If the crust is slashed, the loaf is known as a *snijder*.

Pan bread is baked in various models. The most popular type is the straight-sided tin which gives a loaf that is higher than it is wide. The top crust is usually left untouched to dome in the oven or it can be made into *knipbrood* (snip or scissor bread). As its name suggests, the top crust is snipped at regular intervals with scissors so that the crust of the baked loaf sprawls outwards in two rows of parallel peaks. The larger surface area exposed in this way gives a lot more crust than a rounded loaf. *Boerenbrood* (peasant bread) is baked in a wider, flatter tin so it ends up squatter in shape. *Casinobrood* is Pullman bread, baked in a closed (Pullman or sandwich) tin that is square in section and has a removable lid so that as the dough rises it presses against all four sides of the mould. The top crust is as flat as the bottom and sides. *Lampionbrood* is baked in a ribbed cylindrical tin which opens lengthwise so that the dough can be put into the bottom half and is then closed to allow the dough to fill the mould. Both these shapes yield uniformly square or round slices of bread, making them popular for sandwiches.

All these shapes of loaf can be further distinguished by a topping of some kind. The most popular are grain flakes, coarse cornmeal, sunflower seeds, sesame and poppy seed, and a ground rice topping which bursts as the loaf rises and gives *tijgerbrood* (tiger bread) with a cracked tiger-like pattern. Toppings and shapes can be varied or combined at will and the loaves themselves can be made from wholemeal or white flour or a mixture of the two or, to a lesser extent, rye. The *Zuidlaarderbol* and *Tulband* in this chapter have a specific recipe/shape relation, as do the *Bolus* buns. The chapter on seasonal baking at the end of the book (page 143) describes several traditionally-shaped breads.

What the Dutch eat on their bread

As a necessary foundation to 'bread and ...', many people nowadays spread their bread with butter, though disappointingly, in a country which boasts dairy products of such a high quality, even more with margarine. Still, for the sake of convenience, let us refer to it as 'buttering' bread. The buttering of bread in Holland dates in all likelihood from the Middle Ages.[57] Butter was used for cooking much earlier than as a spread and appeared in an apothecary's book in 1571 as a medicinal item.[58] There were several qualities, the best to be found on the tables in wealthy households and the most inferior, inedible, kinds were commonly used as grease. The use of butter with cheese was greatly discouraged among several social classes as an unnecessary extravagance and the saying *'Zuivel op zuivel, is het werk van de duivel,'* (Dairy food on top of dairy food is the Devil's work), was often eagerly proffered as a justification. In the seventeenth

Jan, the cheese-monger in our home village. He sells wholesale and retail and keeps and matures the cheeses in his own warehouse. Here he is wiping and turning them, a weekly task.

century, butter was a prized export, sent not only to other European countries, but to Africa, Indonesia and the rest of Asia.[59] Generally, the best qualities would be exported and cheaper kinds would be imported for the domestic market.[60] Farmers who produced butter kept enough for their own use but this was usually generously salted to help keep the amount used to a minimum.[61] Those who couldn't afford butter made do with dry bread or used lard, dripping or molasses,[62] and sometimes mixtures of these, pungent flavours which had the added advantage of disguising the lack of a final and appetizing topping. A sampler of Dutch favourites, all essentials to those *broodmaaltijden* that I mentioned earlier, follows.

Cheese

Cheese, which almost certainly predates butter, has been eaten at all levels of society since the Middle Ages and there appears to have been great variety even then.[63] Medieval manuscripts often included recipes that required soft cheeses, which were easy to make at home, while the harder cheeses were more a specialist product and were made on farms. The cheese trade appears to have been at one of its highest points in the sixteenth century and Amsterdam boasted the most important dairy market.[64] Many still-life paintings of the time prominently display wheels of cheese but tastes differed then as much as they still do. Two prominent physicians, van Beverwijck and Blankaart, offered opposing opinions;[65] van Beverwijck much preferred soft creamy cheese made from whole milk and sensibly despised the most mature, worm-ridden sorts. Blankaart was decidedly partial to a good piece of mature cheese, obviously having a different cheesemonger to his colleague. Some people approached the

32

matter with a more open mind, and the household accounts of a seven-teenth-century clergyman show that *'witte, koeye, groene, soetemelcx en witte saen'* (white, cows', green, sweet milk and white cream) cheeses were eaten at his table.[66] Around the same time, the evening meal of Leiden students consisted of buttered bread and cumin-flavoured cheese,[67] a type still called *'Leidse'* today. Of course, not everybody was fortunate enough to enjoy cheese in large quantities and the firmer cheeses were often grated onto bread to stretch them.[68]

Although the average Dutchman loves cheese of almost any kind, he retains a special affection for those of his native country. There is certainly enough variety. Beyond our borders, the round *Edammer* is perhaps the best known. It weighs 1–2 kilos and is usually covered with red wax for export. Its fat content, lower than *Goudse*, enhances its shelf-life and exportability. Gouda cheese comes in wheels weighing 4–20 kilos and while most of it is factory-produced, it is still possible to buy farmhouse Gouda in many places. Gouda-type cheese is often flavoured: *Friese nagelkaas*, Frisian clove cheese, is studded with whole cloves; *kruidenkaas* is speckled with the herbs of its name; *mosterdkaas* is riddled with mustard seeds; *Leidse kaas*, mentioned before, is flavoured with whole cumin seeds. *Maaslander* is similar to Gouda with a sweeter taste and *Leerdammer* is often referred to as 'Dutch hole cheese' as it has an appearance similar to Emmentaler. *Kollumer* is made from unpasteurized milk and *Kernhem* is a small orange-coated wheel which is prized as a dessert cheese. Sheep's or goats' milk cheeses are made on many farms as well as commercially. *Limburgse geitenkaas* is a strong-smelling (to put it mildly) goats' milk cheese, while *Texelaar* is a sheep's milk cheese from the island of Texel. *Graskaas* is a rich-coloured cheese made from the milk of cows that have grazed in pasture after the winter. It is usually eaten while it is still young and soft. Gouda-type and other firm cheeses come in a variety of ages, from 4–10 weeks for *jonge kaas* (young cheese) to at least a year for *overjarige kaas* (over-aged cheese), with several categories in between. The range of flavours is wide and most people have a favourite kind which they prefer at a particular state of maturity.

Fish

Fish was eaten on a far wider scale in the past. Take as an example its popularity as as a breakfast dish in the sixteenth century.[69] Fried fish was particularly popular and fried smelt was given the nickname 'breakfast fish'. Smoked herring, another breakfast favourite, was referred to as 'poor man's bacon'.[70] Pickled herring could be found in any meal in the eighteenth century,[71] and there was an extensive herring fishery dating from at the very least the seventeenth.[72] *Maatjesharing* continues to be a national speciality. The young herring are given enough time at the feeding grounds for their fat content to rise dramatically, giving them a melt-in-the-mouth quality. They are lightly salted and frozen at sea and sold to fishmongers by the cask. The fishmonger skins and fillets them in a special way, leaving the fillets attached at the tail. These herrings are delicious on rolls with a little chopped onion, but another traditional way to eat them is to hold a herring by the tail, dip it in chopped onion, throw your head back and lower it bit by bit into your mouth. I have seen men eat a herring at one gulp, quite like seals at the zoo. It often provokes malicious amusement to see foreign visitors eat and enjoy a *maatjesharing*, only to start to gag when they are told that the herring is actually raw. Dutch smoked eels are popular the world over, and particularly so in Holland, but are still something of a luxury. Fresh and preserved fish can be readily bought from fishmongers and supermarkets as well as from the numerous mobile vending points which travel from place to place on an appointed day. They do a roaring trade in freshly fried fish (no chips – you eat it without or take it home to eat it on bread), from mussels to fish roe, to a fillet of your choice, to the amazingly popular *kibbeling*, marinated chunks of cod or haddock.

Meats

Home-slaughtering, traditionally done in November, is now almost a thing of the past, practised only on a small scale in some country parishes. Once the better cuts of meat had been prepared, offal and remnants were made into a variety of dishes destined to supplement the main meal or to be used as accompaniments to bread. *Balkenbrij* is made from pork offal which is boiled, finely ground and mixed with flour, fat and spices. It is cooked to a stiff porridge and left to set in a suitable container. Once it has set, it can be thickly sliced and fried. *Rolpens* (rather off-puttingly, 'rolled gut') is made from coarsely ground meat, usually including bacon. It is seasoned, stuffed into a length of intestine and then boiled and pickled in vinegar, to be cut and fried later. *Hoofdkaas* and *zure zult* (brawn or head cheese) are similar to each other. A pig's head and trotters, or more rarely a calf's head, are boiled until very tender. The meat is removed and mixed with gherkins, spices, vinegar and enough of the stock to moisten it. It is simmered for a short period then pressed into moulds, covered with a layer of lard and allowed to set. Some recipes call for steeping in brine or vinegar. It is eaten cold. These kinds of homely cut can be bought from butchers and some supermarkets but must compete very strongly with the dozens of kinds of smoked and boiled hams, both domestic and imported, and the whole end-less of array of cold cuts made from pork, beef, lamb and chicken, some traditional, others invented almost weekly by manufacturers. *Rookvlees*, smoked beef, is one of the traditional kinds. In the past it was often cured at home, wrapped in cloth and hung in the chimney. It was apparently recognized abroad as a Dutch delicacy, and the English cookery book by Eliza Smith *The Compleat Housewife*, first published in 1727, gives a recipe for 'Dutch Beef'.[73]

The Dutch *slaatje*

The chilling cabinets and deli-counters of supermarkets house large varieties of *slaatjes*, mayonnaise-based salads in several flavours. These salads tend to rely heavily on potato to give them body, though with the obvious exception of potato salad, you can never actually put your finger on a piece of potato as it is all a homogeneous mass. Tinned fish like salmon and tuna are pressed into use, while the top end of the market includes crab and shrimp. Chicken is becoming increasingly popular, the dressing flavoured in a number of exotic ways; even egg salad can be bought prepared. *Huzarensalade* is flavoured with shredded cooked meat and is a firm favourite. These salads are usually bought in a plastic dish, to be eaten with a fork or to be scooped out onto bread, but for special occasions they can be heaped on a platter, slathered with yet more mayonnaise and decorated with pickles, asparagus, stuffed eggs and tomatoes and in the case of fish salads, bits of smoked fish. They form a centrepiece which gradually collapses as more people people scoop out a portion to eat on a slice of crusty bread. This *slaatje* is an amazing phenomenon. I have never understood why they sell so well in a nation that is noted for its often frugal ways with food. The ingredients are all store-cupboard staples and leftover bits and pieces which can be put together in a few minutes at the most, with the added advantage that you can give the preservatives and flavour enhancers a miss. Nevertheless, I and people like me who whip up our own, remain in the minority.

Sweet accompaniments

Stroop, molasses, was one of the earliest sweet accompaniments and remains popular, though more so as a pancake-topping than on bread. It was used as a sweetener and flavouring agent in porridges and gruels as well as a spread for bread and pancakes, and this cheap refinery by-product was a valuable source of iron, particularly for the poor in whose diets it figured most prominently. The quantity used varied greatly and at times it amounted almost to abuse. In the eighteenth century, on the island of Marken, north of Amsterdam, it was not uncommon for a family to get though 100–150 kilos in a year.[74] Apples and pears were also boiled down to a syrupy consistency and black-strap colour and used like molasses, a Limburger tradition which can be traced back at least to the seventeenth century. It started out as a cottage industry which became industrialized at the end of the nineteenth century.

Jam, originally a delicacy enjoyed by the wealthy, was made more accessible from 1885 when the first jam factory was founded, fittingly enough at the heart of the fruit-growing region, not fifteen kilometres from where I live. The industry was greatly stimulated during the First World War when the export market for fruit dried up.[75]

Chocolate specialities like *hagelslag*, chocolate vermicelli, are loved by young and old and contemporary versions include not only the obligatory milk and semi-sweet, but mocha, extra bitter and even single-crop varieties for the more discerning palate. The Dutch version of the American staple, peanut butter and jelly sandwiches, is peanut butter and *hagelslag*. *Vlokken*, chocolate ribbons, has its adherents but has never been as popular as *hagelslag*. Chocolate-coated puffed rice is a recent innovation and choco-late paste in several flavours continues to hold its own. *Kokosbrood*, coconut bread, which is like coconut ice, is sliced wafer thin and sold in packages of plain or mixed flavours. If you buy it from the healthfood department it will contain all natural ingredients and no preservatives. The highly-flavoured variations – pistachio, strawberry, banana – are loved by children. *Muisjes*, sugar-coated aniseed, which are described more fully in the chapter on rusks on page 59, are eaten year-round by many people. *Gestampte muisjes*, powdered *muisjes* originally manufactured for those whose teeth were not up to dealing with the whole seeds, are perhaps even more popular on bread than the whole seeds which are eaten on rusks.

COARSE RYE BREAD
Roggebrood

Until the Second World War, coarse rye bread continued to form the mainstay of Dutch people's diets, though less so for those living in the west of the country and in Zeeland. It had actually been losing some of its popularity before the war, but as rye was more readily available during the war itself than wheat, its decline was delayed. The western provinces had no firm grain-growing tradition, so there was no suggestion of self-sufficiency fixing eating habits, as was very much the case in the predominantly agriculturally inclined north, south and east. Zeeland had a well-established reputation for growing good wheat – up to today 'Zeeland flour' is a bakery expression used to denote wheat flour with specific properties – and its inhabitants, accustomed as they were to eating wheaten bread, despised coarse rye bread as being fit only for live-stock fodder.[76] They, like the rest of Holland, baked rye bread expressly for their cows, horses and even dogs.[77] These loaves were made from poor quality rye which was not usually picked over or even properly sifted. The poorest of the poor sometimes used this meal to make bread for themselves. This was particularly the case in the east of the country with the result that sand colic, an illness practically unknown elsewhere, reared its head there from time to time.[78]

Much of the rye used was homegrown, but some still had to be imported to meet the demand. There were those who swore by the softer local grain, deeming it far tastier. Others prized St Petersburg rye for its powers of water-absorption.[79] Those who grew rye took it to be milled and baked their own bread from it. Sometimes a sack of rye meal would be left with a local baker, from which he would be expected to make bread for its owner. Many a country baker, eking out a meagre existence, was charged with the extra burden of keeping everybody's rye separate and kneading several batches of dough. An alternative was for customers to bring their loaves to be baked in his oven. Even though this involved less work, it must have had him tearing his hair out in frustration, because he would be given loaves not only of varying consistency but also of varying size. There was usually a flat baking fee per loaf, so the more cunning didn't scruple to bring single loaves weighing 10–15 kilos.[80]

The best course was for the baker to keep the complete production process in his own hands, when he would make the coarse rye loaves four or five times a week, alternating with the finer articles which were less in demand. An average oven would take about 400 kilos of dough. The dough would be kneaded in a huge wooden trough, though 'treaded' would be

The morning's work at our local bakery. Here a modern deck oven is charged with tin loaves. They are put on the cooling racks which can then be wheeled to wherever is most convenient.

more accurate. The first dough-kneader was invented in 1603, expressly for avoiding foot contact and thereby rendering it more palatable in the inventor's view,[81] but it wasn't until the beginning of the twentieth century that machines – dog-, horse- and petrol-powered – gained popularity, especially in rural areas. Using the feet was the easiest way to knead the heavy dough efficiently, making full use of one's weight. The modern mind finds this distasteful; not so the customer of old. As one former baker recounts, a customer complained at the beginning that the bread had a machine taste, whereupon the baker tartly rejoined that at least the sweaty foot aroma was gone.[82] Admittedly, both body temperature and physical contact have a beneficial effect on dough – but of course one would prefer the contact to be manual in the true sense of the word.

Nowadays most of the coarse rye bread is produced industrially. Modern machines, ovens and production processes have accustomed us to the uniform little slabs of thinly-sliced bread with a consistent taste. This was not always so. The best rye breads were baked in stone-floored ovens, and the choice of fuel greatly influenced the flavour. Wood, twigs, shavings, sawdust, oil and peat were all used, but seldom coal as it gave an unpleasant taste. The dough was removed from the trough with an iron spade and shaped into bricklike loaves. They would either be placed in a large wooden mould which accommodated several loaves, or extra dough would be plastered around the outer sides of the batch to help the loaves keep their shape and texture. This insulating dough would be crumbled into the following batch or used as animal fodder.[83] The oven door would often be plastered with more dough to keep out draughts. The mortar-like qualities of rye dough had apparently been recognized for hundreds of years. It is said to have been used to hold the bricks of more than one building together.[84] The baked dough was often used as a household remedy too: mixed with mustard and vinegar it made a poultice that cured things as diverse as headaches and fevers.[85]

The loaves have to be baked for several hours, and the gradually diminishing heat of the old ovens had a beneficial effect. Moisture is also essential and while some bakers threw a few wet sacks onto the loaves, others opted for a more practical approach, neatly killing two birds with one stone. A large stockpot, sometimes with a few pulses or root vegetables added, would be put into the oven, creating a moist atmosphere and yielding a delicious soup.[86]

There has always been great regional diversity, persisting even in the face of mass-production. The best-known type is perhaps the Frisian rye bread. This is one of the darkest and coarsest kinds and it is usually made from a mixture of domestic and foreign grain.[87] The coarsely crushed rye is mixed with water and salt and a part of it is put in what are known as sweetening pans in a very slow oven, usually overnight. This subtle heat treatment serves to convert some of the starch into sugars, giving the bread its characteristic sweetish taste – sometimes heightened with a little malt extract. If old bread is to be used as part of the fresh dough (a universal practice in Dutch and German rye-bread baking), it is crumbled and soaked in water for several hours. The contents of the sweetening pan are mixed with the boiled-up old bread and the remaining, freshly mixed dough, then the loaves are shaped, rolled in rye bran, brushed with a flour paste and baked for a few hours to form a crust. The temperature is then lowered and the loaves are baked for a further 10–20 hours in a slow oven. The loaves

More work at the baker's bench. From the top: loaves are given their second proof on the work-top; the baker reshapes them; they are quickly rolled in bran; and laid on a tray ready for baking.

containing crumbled bread are generally baked for a longer time and are darker in colour than the others.

Groningen rye bread is made similarly but is usually baked for 10–12 hours and is a bit sweeter.[88] In Limburg the bread is far lighter in colour and is also less compact than the two types already mentioned. It is made from finely ground rye and a sourdough starter;[89] sometimes a little yeast is added. The baking time is also far shorter, only 2–3 hours. Brabant rye bread is yet lighter in structure, owing to the addition of a small proportion of wheat flour.[90] In Gelderland, two kinds of rye bread are made, both sourdough and unsoured. For the sourdough a fairly soft dough made from finely ground rye and water is left to develop for one or more days. Salt and more meal are added to make a firm dough which is shaped into loaves, rolled in rye bran and brushed with a flour paste, then baked for about 13 hours. For the sweet loaves the dough is not left to ripen and a little yeast is sometimes added.[91] Two lesser-known types are Amsterdam Black and Hague Sweet. Coarsely ground rye and molasses form the basis of Amsterdam Black and the rye bran in which the moulded dough is rolled is toasted first. The loaves are baked for about 24 hours. Hague Sweet is baked for about 16 hours and, instead of molasses, colourless glucose syrup is used.[92]

Baking the rye loaves described here is such a specialist task that most are produced industrially and sold pre-packaged in supermarkets. Few bakers are prepared to make them in the way they should be, so some ignore them while others buy them from one of the artisanal bakeries that specialize in making the local varieties. Healthfood shops tend to sell the best ones.

ROUND BUTTERMILK RYE LOAF
Karnemelkse roggebol

The buttermilk in this loaf gives it the deliciously tart taste usually associated with sourdough rye breads. But it doesn't need a starter and is very simple to make. It is quite the trend at the moment for bakers to use tangy ingredients like buttermilk and curd cheese in breads, particularly during the warmer months. Effective advertising campaigns send customers scuttling in droves to bakeries, dying to be refreshed by such cool-sounding ingredients. Buttermilk was used quite extensively in the past. In rural societies where wastefulness and displays of abundance were frowned upon, it was quite acceptable to use buttermilk, a by-product of butter-churning which might otherwise be fed to the livestock. It was the liquid of choice in rye breads from Gelderland,[93] and in Zeeland many farmers who took their own wheat to the baker often took along a jug of fresh buttermilk to mix into the dough, giving the bread a delicious tang and improving its keeping qualities.[94] In the northern province of Drenthe in the nineteenth century, most peasants baked their bread at home in outdoor ovens. The rye would be ground and sifted, then used to make three qualities of bread, from coarse to fine. Buttermilk was generally added to the dough.[95] It is sometimes difficult to find buttermilk in British shops. You can mix a pint of skimmed milk with a teaspoon of cream of tartar as an approximate substitute.

Sourdough is used in few Dutch breads and crops up mainly along the Dutch-German border as well as in some coarse rye breads that need a slight lift. Beyond this region, mainstream bakeries tend largely to ignore such loaves but healthfood stores carry good selections. During the Second World War, sourdough was often used in wheaten bread, to stretch what little yeast was available.[96] People never like to be reminded of deprivation, so that might account for the lack of post-war fondness for natural leavens. The new generation, however, has taken a fresh approach and there is increasing awareness and appreciation of once-despised flavours.

Oven: 220°C ♦ Tin: baking sheet ♦ Time: 25–30 minutes

350g strong white flour	*1 tsp sugar*
150g rye flour	*1 tsp salt*
1 $^1/_4$ tsp easyblend yeast	*approx. 325 ml buttermilk, warmed slightly*

Put the flours, yeast, sugar and salt in a large bowl. Add the buttermilk and mix with a spoon or spatula until the dry ingredients are well moistened. Turn out onto a lightly-floured surface and knead until elastic. The dough is quite sticky which is characteristic of rye doughs, but it responds well to kneading. Shape into a ball and place in a large bowl. Cover with a tea towel wrung out in hot water and leave in a warm draught-free place until doubled in bulk.

Knock back the risen dough and transfer to a well-floured surface. Flour your hands well and knead until once more elastic. Shape into a ball and place on a well-floured baking sheet. Dust liberally with rye flour and cover loosely with unoiled clingfilm. Place in a warm draught-free place until almost doubled in size. Bake for 25–30 minutes. The loaf should sound hollow when tapped. Cool on a wire rack. Serve thinly sliced. This loaf is excellent with cold cuts.

MULTIGRAIN BREAD
Meergranenbrood

The combination of coarse meals and sunflower seeds gives a marvellous texture and this loaf stays moist for a few days. It is by nature quite compact but a few bakers add gluten powder to their dough to make it lighter and more voluminous, part of the unfathomable desire for uniformity that some of them seem to have. Although mixed-grain breads have been popular for centuries, cornmeal is a relative newcomer. The stigma surrounding its introduction in the nineteenth century as animal fodder delayed its acceptance as fit sustenance for humans, among whom it has become quite popular in the past few decades.

Oven: 220°C ♦ Tin: 1250 ml loaf tin ♦ Time: 25–30 minutes

100g wholewheat flour	*2 tsp sugar*
100g strong white flour	*$^3/_4$ tsp salt*
100g wholemeal rye flour	*approx. 250 ml milk, warmed*
100g coarse cornmeal (polenta)	*50g butter, melted*
1 $^3/_4$ tsp easyblend yeast	*100g sunflower seeds*

Put the flours, cornmeal, yeast, sugar and salt in a large bowl. Add the milk and butter and mix with a spoon or spatula until the dry ingredients are well moistened. Turn out onto a lightly-floured surface and knead until elastic. This dough is moister than average but try not to add too much extra flour while kneading. Knead in the sunflower seeds. Shape into a ball and place in a large bowl. Cover with a tea towel wrung out in hot water and leave in a warm draught-free place until doubled in bulk.

Knock back the risen dough and transfer to a lightly-floured surface. Knead well and roll out, or thoroughly flatten with your hands, to a rectangle measuring about 20 x 30 cm. Roll up tightly from one short end. Pinch the edges to seal and place in the tin with the seam centred at the bottom. Cover with lightly-oiled clingfilm and leave in a warm draught-free place until almost doubled in size. Bake for about 25 to 30 minutes. The loaf should sound hollow when tapped with the knuckles. Cool on a wire rack.

Three loaves of spiced bread from Zeeland: coming to the end of its first rise; moulded and left to prove in the tins; out of the oven and on to the cooling rack.

SPICED BREAD FROM ZEELAND
Zeeuws Kruidbrood

This subtly spiced bread is eaten in some parts of Zeeland on special occasions.

Oven: 220°C ♦ Tin: 1250ml loaf tin ♦ Time: 25–30 minutes

350g strong white flour	pinch of mace
1 $\frac{1}{4}$ tsp easyblend yeast	2 tsp whole aniseed
2 tbsp sugar	approx. 200 ml milk, warmed
$\frac{3}{4}$ tsp salt	50g butter, melted
$\frac{1}{4}$ tsp freshly grated nutmeg	75g candied citron, chopped (optional)

Put the flour, yeast, sugar, salt, nutmeg, mace and aniseed in a large bowl. Add the milk and butter and mix with a spoon or spatula until the dry ingredients are well moistened. Turn out onto a lightly-floured surface and knead until elastic. Knead in the citron towards the end. Shape into a ball and place in a large bowl. Cover with a tea towel wrung out in hot water and leave in a warm draught-free place until doubled in bulk.

Knock back the risen dough. Knead well and roll out, or thoroughly flatten with your hands to a rectangle about 20 x 30 cm. Roll up tightly from one short end. Pinch the edges to seal and place in the tin with the seam centred at the bottom. Cover with lightly-oiled clingfilm and leave in a warm draught-free place until almost doubled in size. Bake for 25–30 minutes. The loaf should sound hollow when tapped with the knuckles. Cool on a wire rack.

SUGAR BREAD
Suikerbrood

Suikerbrood, or *sukerbole* as it is called in Frisian, is a Frisian speciality made with sugar chips or sugar cubes which dissolve into delicious little craters throughout the loaf. Sugar cubes are easier to come by and are not as ruinous to dental work as the harder chips which take longer to dissolve. Another version of this loaf is made in Brabant where it is known as *klontjesmik*.

Oven: 220°C ♦ Tin: 1250 ml loaf tin, lined ♦ Time: 20–25 minutes

350g strong white flour
1 ¹/₂ tsp easyblend yeast
1 ¹/₂ tbsp sugar
³/₄ tsp salt
2 tsp cinnamon (optional)

approx. 200 ml milk, warmed
75g butter, melted
100–125g sugar cubes, broken
into pieces and sifted
free of fine particles,
or loaf sugar chips

Put the flour, yeast, sugar, salt and cinnamon in a large bowl. Add the milk and butter and mix with a spoon or spatula until the dry ingredients are well moistened. Turn out onto a lightly-floured surface and knead until elastic. Shape into a ball and place in a large bowl. Cover with a tea towel wrung out in hot water and leave in a warm draught-free place until doubled in bulk.

Knock back the dough and knead until once more elastic. Knead the sugar as evenly as possible into the dough. Roll or thoroughly flatten into a rectangle about 20 x 30 cm. Try to get all of the sugar sealed in by dough to avoid scorching. Roll up tightly from one short end. Pinch the ends together to seal. Place the roll into the lined tin, with the seam centred at the bottom of the tin. Cover loosely with lightly-oiled clingfilm and leave in a warm, draught-free place until almost doubled in bulk. Bake for about 25 minutes. When tapped with the knuckles the loaf should sound hollow. Remove the lining paper and cool on a wire rack. Eat sliced with butter.

CURRANT BREAD WITH ALMOND PASTE
Krentenbrood met spijs

Dutch fruit loaves tend to put the sparsely populated loaves of other countries in the shade. Bakers vie with each other to stuff their loaves to bursting with fruit, nuts, citron and peels and it is a miserly baker who dares to use less than an equal amount of fruit to flour. This has given rise to a colloquial expression, *krenterig*, from the word for currant, meaning really stingy, and woe betide the baker whose customers put it about that one has to cycle from one currant to the next in his bread. The only case in which a restrained hand with the fruit is accepted is in the almost forgotten *vliegenbrood*, 'fly bread', which used to be baked for Good Friday in western Holland; the sprinkling of currants against the background of dough gave it its name. Fruit breads were once eaten only on festive occasions but they have now become staples. The variety in texture is stunning: they are made from white, wholewheat or rye flour, as well as mixtures of these, and the *roggeknar* is a coarse rye bread with a filling of fruit and nuts. Currant bread with a roll of almond paste baked into it is a typical weekend treat. The way you eat it undoubtedly says a lot about your personality. You can eat it buttered, eating the edges first and saving the almond-paste bit for last, or you can butter it and excavate the almond paste to spread on top of the butter. Whichever way you choose, it's delicious.

Oven: 200°C ♦ Tin: 1250ml loaf tin ♦ Time: 30–35 minutes

250g strong white flour	50g butter, melted
1 tsp easyblend yeast	1 egg, lightly beaten
2 tbsp sugar	125g currants
$1/_2$ tsp salt	75g sultanas
zest of $1/_2$ lemon	150g almond paste
approx. 80 ml milk, warmed	a little beaten egg as needed

Put the flour, yeast, sugar, salt and lemon zest in a large bowl. Add the milk, butter and beaten egg and mix with a spoon or spatula until the dry ingredients are well moistened. Turn out onto a lightly-floured surface and knead until elastic. Shape into a ball and return to the bowl. Cover with a tea towel wrung out in hot water and leave in a warm draught-free place until doubled in bulk.

While the dough is rising put the currants and raisins in a bowl and cover with hot water. Mix the almond paste with enough egg to make it just malleable. Shape it into a sausage about 17 cm long and set aside. Knock

47

back the risen dough and transfer to a lightly-floured surface. Drain the fruit and pat dry with kitchen paper or a clean tea towel. Knead it into the dough. Don't be discouraged by the ominous squelching sound and the initial reluctance of the fruit to blend into the dough. Persevere and you will be rewarded with a smooth soft dough and well-distributed fruit. Roll out or thoroughly flatten with your hands to a rectangle about 20 x 30 cm. Place the almond paste about two centimetres from one short end and roll it tightly into the dough. Pinch the edges to seal and place in the tin with the seam centred at the bottom. Cover with lightly-oiled clingfilm and leave in a warm draught-free place until almost doubled in size. Bake for 30–35 minutes. The loaf should sound hollow when tapped with the knuckles. Cool on a wire rack.

MOULDED YEAST RING
Tulband *or* Boffert

The *tulband* resembles the Alsatian *Gugelhupf* in consistency and shape and takes its name from the mould, called a *tulband* or turban. *Tulbanden* have long been popular as a celebration yeast cake, although the name is often used nowadays to describe a cake-batter version which is also baked in a turban mould; it generally contains chopped fruit like most of the older types. To confuse matters a bit, the same yeast cake is referred to as *boffert* in some places in Friesland.[97] In most of the rest of Holland a *boffert*, *poffert* or *broeder* is a fairly compact stove-top pudding made from a yeast batter. These puddings have been popular for centuries and are well-represented in eighteenth-century cookery books.[98] In the seventeenth century a dish known as *pofferbroodt* often accompanied the array of sweet and savoury pies and tarts served with the third course in wealthy homes.[99] Its social role changed over the centuries and by the twentieth century it occupied various places on the menu: some ate it as a main dish while others preferred it as a side dish with pulses or as a dessert.[100] Its modern role, when nostalgia conjures it up, is generally as a dessert and it is usually made from a mixture of buckwheat and wheat, with dried fruit and sometimes a little bacon, served warm with melted butter or with a warm sauce made from dripping and molasses. The dough is put in a heavy pan with a generous amount of dripping or lard and turned over once during cooking, when it has browned on one side. The same mixture can also be put in a covered pudding-mould to steam, and becomes *ketelkoek*, or it can be wrapped in a cloth and boiled. This version, called *Jan-in-de-zak* (John-in-the-bag), is first cousin to Spotted Dick. In north Holland there is a variant of the *broeder*, the *Hoornse broeder*, which originated in the town of Hoorn. It is a rich round fruit loaf made by spreading a mixture of brown sugar, cinnamon and butter on a circular piece of dough and topping it with a second circle. Traditionally, it was served at the birth of a baby, but nowadays it is popular for all sorts of occasions.

But to get back to the *tulband*, it was generally eaten at celebrations and in its old-fashioned yeast form it is often found today in the festive December season. It formed part of Frisian celebratory meals, as described in an account from the mid-nineteenth century, and supposedly came from the baker.[101] In Zeeland it was often baked at home and was invariably served at weddings. The moulds were made of glazed brown earthenware and a little cake was made together with the larger one. There were two versions, plain or with raisins and chopped citron. After baking, the large cake was decorated with what was charmingly referred to as 'rat droppings' in the Cadzand area, elongated boiled sugar sweets which were stuck into the cake, and it was generously dusted with laboriously home-ground powdered sugar. The small cake was placed on top and decorated with a paper flower. There was a serving ritual. The small cake was given to the youngest guests. Then the large cake was cut horizontally at the point where the 'band' of the turban joins the swirly part. The two pieces were cut into wedges, buttered liberally and sprinkled with sugar and accompanied with cups of tea.[102]

The yeast *tulband* has changed little over the years as a mid-nineteenth-century recipe shows.[103] This is for a rich plain yeast cake made with 250g flour, 150g butter and 50g sugar, enriched with eggs and milk and flavoured with lemon zest. In the following recipe very ordinary ingredients metamorphose into a beautifully textured flavourful cake, in the peasant tradition.

Oven: 200°C ♦ Tin: tulband or other ring mould, 2 l capacity, well greased
Time: 35–40 minutes

500g strong white flour	150g butter, melted
2 ¹/₂ tsp easyblend yeast	2 eggs, lightly beaten
50g sugar	150g currants
1 tsp salt	150g sultanas
zest of 1 lemon	50g chopped citron (optional)
approx. 200 ml milk, warmed	icing sugar for dusting

Put the flour, yeast, sugar, salt and lemon zest in a large bowl. Add the milk, butter and beaten egg and mix with a spoon or spatula until the dry ingredients are well moistened. Turn out onto a floured surface and knead until elastic. This is a soft dough that responds well to kneading. Shape into a ball and place in a large bowl. Cover with a tea towel wrung out in hot water and leave in a warm draught-free place until doubled in bulk.

While the dough is rising put the currants and sultanas in a bowl and cover with hot water. Knock back the risen dough and transfer to a lightly-floured surface. Drain the fruit and pat dry with kitchen paper or a clean tea towel and knead it into the dough. Try to get all of the fruit well-embedded in the dough as pieces that are loose on the surface will scorch during baking. Shape into a ball and use your fingers to make a hole in the centre, large enough to fit neatly over the central tube of the tin. Place in the tin and cover with lightly-oiled clingfilm. Leave in a warm draught-free place until almost doubled in size. Bake for 35–40 minutes. The loaf should sound hollow when tapped with the knuckles. Cool on a wire rack. Dust with icing sugar before serving.

The 800th annual horse market at Zuidlaren, where an estimated 2000 horses change hands and, more to the point, 100,000 Zuidlaarderbollen fly across the counters. The whole town gets in on the act: the chemist and greengrocer, as well as the baker, have their own stalls. And if a loaf is more than you can handle, a girl will sell you buttered slices.

ROUND FRUIT LOAF FROM ZUIDLAREN
Zuidlaarderbol

The rye flour gives this fruit loaf a lovely flavour and keeps it very moist for several days. It comes from Zuidlaren in the northern province of Drenthe where every year on the third Tuesday in October, the oldest and most famous horse market in western Europe is held, a tradition which dates from around 1200. Local bakers bake it all year round, but the fair turnover is truly amazing. As the third Tuesday in October rolls around, Zuidlaren starts gearing itself up for the market. For this day at least, the town lives and breathes horseflesh and *Zuidlaarderbollen*. While about 2,000 horses change hands, an incredible 100,000 loaves find willing buyers and the whole town appears to work indefatigably to this end. The normally tranquil town is transformed for the day. Grass verges and large empty spaces accommodate cars and bicycles and youngsters hover around importantly, enjoying their semi-official status as parking attendants as much as they delight in a day off from their schoolwork. There is a fun-fair in the main square and the side streets house neat ranks of beautiful horses and ponies. The main street is lined with stalls selling *Zuidlaarderbollen*. As far as the eye can see, row upon endless row of loaves is displayed and even the two local bakers set up extra sales points outside to supplement the brisk business they do indoors. Sample wedges of *bol* slathered with butter are hospitably pressed on passers-by and, after tasting them, few can resist buying at least one loaf to take home. Those who search for a shop to buy a roll of film, a bunch of bananas or a bottle of shampoo will do so in vain. Regular business is firmly pushed into the background and most shop doors are kept resolutely shut. Instead, you will find photographer, greengrocer and chemist alike plying a vigorous trade in *Zuidlaarder-bollen*, competing for customers with local charities and professional market-folk. Any spare bit of space is cordoned off and pressed into use. Impromptu teashops and refreshment stands abound and people sit contentedly munching on bits of *bol* and sipping coffee, comfortable for the moment in plastic garden chairs or on bales of hay – an authentic touch which reminds one that the occasion is primarily a horse market, however prominently the *Zuidlaarderbol* may feature.

Oven: 220°C ♦ Tin: large sheet, dusted with flour ♦ Time: 25–30 minutes
Yield: 2 loaves

250g strong white flour	*approx. 250 ml milk, warmed*
250g rye flour	*50g butter, melted*
2 ¹/₄ tsp easyblend yeast	*1 egg, lightly beaten*
1 tbsp sugar	*150g raisins*
1 tsp salt	*150g currants*
50g candied citron, chopped	

Put the flours, yeast, sugar and salt in a large bowl. Add the milk, butter and beaten egg and mix with a spoon or spatula until the dry ingredients are well moistened. Turn out onto a floured surface and knead until elastic. The dough is quite sticky because of the rye flour but it soon responds to your hands so try not to add extra flour while kneading. Shape into a ball and place in a large bowl. Cover with a tea towel wrung out in hot water and leave in a warm draught-free place until doubled in bulk.

While the dough is rising put the raisins and currants in a bowl and cover with hot water. Knock back the risen dough and transfer to a floured surface. Drain the fruit and pat dry with kitchen paper or a clean tea towel. Knead it into the dough along with the citron. The dough will feel very slippery under your hands as it comes into contact with the fruit but keep on at it! By the time you have kneaded in all the fruit the texture will have improved. Try to get all of the fruit well-embedded in the dough to avoid scorching. Divide the dough into two pieces and shape each into a ball. You will need to flour both your hands and the dough well to be able to handle it properly. Place the balls on the floured sheet. Dust with flour and cover with unoiled clingfilm. Leave in a warm draught-free place for twenty minutes.

Remove the clingfilm and use a sharp knife to cut in to a depth of 1.5 cm around the middle of each loaf, halfway up. Make sure that you use a sharp knife that really cuts into the dough, enabling it to rise properly. Gently flatten the top with your palms and score with a crisscross pattern. Some people slash a Star of David into the loaf instead, a practice which may be based on Solomon's bread stamp.[104] Cover again with clingfilm and leave for a further 20 minutes. Bake for 25–30 minutes. The loaves should sound hollow when tapped with the knuckles. Cool on a wire rack.

BROWN SUGAR COILS
Bolussen

These buns are a traditional speciality from Zeeland but they are now popular all over the country. They can be shaped into figures of eight and are then usually called a Hague *bolus*. Though the name *bolus* is common everywhere, they are sometimes called *jikkemien* in Zeeland or, rather unfortunately, *drollen*. A folklorist,[105] describing Cadzand specialities, suggests rather hopefully that the name comes either from English 'droll' or French '*drôle*'. Humour does come into it, but of a vulgar sort. *Drol* also means turd and, unappetizing though the thought may be, it doesn't take a lot of imagination to see how the name may have come about. The name *bolus* has Spanish connotations and it is possible that a yeast roll of some kind may have been issued to Spanish soldiers stationed in Zeeland during the Eighty Year War (1566–1648). But there is a stronger case for its Jewish origins. While Ashkenazi cuisine also has a bread called *boles*, it is to Sephardic cookery that we must turn for the roots of the Dutch *bolus*. Many Sephardic Jews sought refuge in Amsterdam when Inquisitorial pressure forced them to flee from Spain. They soon founded a thriving community. The two other variants, *bolussen* made with ginger or with almond paste, are firmly rooted in Amsterdam Jewish culture where the ginger *bolus* is still the speciality of a few kosher bakeries.

BASIC BOLUS RECIPE

Oven: 220°C ◆ Tin: Large baking sheet, preferably lined
Time: 12–15 minutes ◆ Yield: 15 buns

500g strong white flour
2 ¹/₂ tsp easyblend yeast
2 tbsp sugar

1 tsp salt
approx. 200 ml milk, warmed
125g butter, melted
1 egg, lightly beaten

Cinnamon sugar:
200g soft dark brown sugar
2 tsp cinnamon

Put the flour, yeast, sugar and salt in a large bowl. Add the milk, butter and beaten egg and mix with a spoon or spatula until the dry ingredients are well moistened. Turn out onto a lightly-floured surface and knead until elastic. Shape into a ball and place in a large bowl. Cover with a tea towel wrung out in hot water and leave in a warm draught-free place until doubled in bulk.

Mix the cinnamon and sugar together and scatter over a large baking sheet (not the one you will be using to bake the buns) or a clean tray. Knock back the dough and knead once more until elastic. Divide into 15 pieces. Shape each piece into a rope about 35 cm long. As soon as each rope is ready, roll it around in the cinnamon sugar and leave on the tin or tray so that it can 'sweat' nicely in the sugar. When you have made all of the ropes you can start shaping them. Twist into loose coils and tuck the end neatly underneath. Arrange on the baking sheet and scatter any remaining sugar over them. Cover loosely with clingfilm and leave in a warm draught-free place until almost doubled in size. Bake for about 12 minutes. Remove immediately from the sheet and cool on a wire rack. Eat fresh or store in an airtight container, or even a plastic bag for a few hours, to let the sugar coating soften to a slight stickiness (which most Dutch people prefer).

GINGER COILS
Gemberbolussen

You have to be very fond of ginger to enjoy this bun. You will need ginger preserved in syrup for this recipe, both the ginger and the syrup.

Oven: 220°C ♦ Time: 20 minutes ♦ Yield: 12
Baking tin: a well-greased bun tin with large cavities, each about 9 cm diameter across, or a large sheet, well greased or lined with non-stick parchment.

$1/_2$ quantity bolus dough (basic recipe)
$1/_2$ amount cinnamon sugar
About 100 ml ginger syrup

Filling:
75g butter, softened
75g caster sugar
150g preserved ginger, very finely chopped

Make the dough as described in the basic recipe. Put the cinnamon sugar on a large spare baking sheet or a clean tray that will accommodate a rolling pin. Cream the butter and sugar for the filling and add the ginger. After proving and re-kneading divide the dough into 12 pieces. Make a rough ball from each piece and roll out in the cinnamon sugar to a rough oval or shoe-sole shape about 18 x 5 cm. Turn over once to coat both sides. Put a thin line of filling in the centre of the rolled-out dough. Moisten the edges of the dough with a little water and pinch to seal, thus enclosing the filling in the dough. Roll this carefully through the cinnamon sugar until it is about 25 cm long. Shape into a knot with one end on top and the other at the bottom. Dip thoroughly in the ginger syrup and arrange in the cavity or on the baking sheet. The bun tin is strongly recommended as it keeps mess to a minimum and conserves more of the ginger syrup. Cover very loosely with lightly-oiled cling-film and leave in a warm, draught-free place again until almost doubled in bulk. Bake for 12–15 minutes. They are best eaten slightly warm.

ALMOND-PASTE COILS
Orgeadebolussen

Orgeade is an old fashioned word for almond paste. I have noticed that many bakers are fond of combining the two fillings – almond paste and ginger – to make a hybrid which they call a Ginger Coil, but they are two distinct products, delicious though the hybrid may be. No ginger syrup is used in this recipe, so it's quite all right to use a baking sheet instead of a bun tin. Dutch Sephardic Jews used to pour a rose-water syrup over the buns, calling them *bole met calder,*[106] *bolus* with bouillon, again betraying a Spanish background (*calder* = *caldo*), even though the bouillon in question is a syrup. Most Jewish recipes still call for the buns to be brushed with syrup after baking.

¹/₂ quantity bolus *dough (basic recipe)*
¹/₂ amount cinnamon sugar

Filling:

150g almond paste
enough beaten egg to make a spreadable paste
which can be forced through a piping bag

Duplicate the process described in the recipe for Ginger Coils, but fill with almond-paste mixture instead of ginger mixture. You can do this with a spoon, guided by your finger, but it is much easier and less messy to use a piping bag fitted with an 8–10 mm nozzle. Make sure they are very well sealed or the filling will leak out as the buns bake. Shape and bake as for Ginger Coils, omitting the ginger syrup stage. Cool on a wire rack.

BRABANT-STYLE SAUSAGE ROLLS
Brabantse Worstenbroodjes

The well-known sausage rolls made from puff pastry which are eaten all over the world are also very popular in Holland but are considered quite commonplace by connoisseurs of the real *worstenbroodjes*, made from a yeast dough with a very generous meat filling. As the name implies, the rolls have their origins in the southern province of Brabant. In Holland ready-ground *half-om-half* – half beef and half pork – mince is generally used. Flavouring tends to be conservative, just salt, pepper and a little nutmeg.

Some bakers use commercial stock-powder as an all-in-one flavouring. If you try this, remember that it is very salty so use it sparingly! Similar rolls are made in Zeeland, though on a far smaller scale than in Brabant. The rolls from Zeeland are filled with lengths of fresh eel, and the ends are left open so that the sharp spine is visible after baking. The rolls are eaten from the side so that the bone can be neatly discarded in one piece.

Oven: 220°C ◆ Tin: baking sheet ◆ Time: 15 minutes ◆ Yield: 20 rolls

Dough:	Filling:
350g strong white flour	*500g minced pork and/or beef*
1 $1/_2$ tsp easyblend yeast	*1 egg, lightly beaten*
2 tsp sugar	*50g fresh white breadcrumbs*
$1/_2$ tsp salt	*a pinch of grated nutmeg*
50g butter, melted	*salt and pepper to taste*
approx. 150 ml milk, warmed	
1 egg, lightly beaten	

Put the flour, yeast, sugar and salt in a large bowl. Add the milk, butter and egg and mix with a spoon or spatula until the dry ingredients are well moistened. Turn out onto a lightly-floured surface and knead until elastic. Shape into a ball and return to the bowl. Cover with a tea towel wrung out in hot water and leave in a warm draught-free place until doubled in bulk.

Mix the ingredients for the filling together. Form 20 sausages about 11 cm long and set aside in a cool place. Knock back the risen dough and transfer to a lightly-floured surface. Knead well. Divide the dough into 20 equal pieces. Roll each piece out to an elongated oval about 15 x 7.5 cm. Put a sausage lengthwise on the centre of the dough. Bring down the dough flaps to cover the top and bottom of the sausage. Roll the rest of the dough around the sausage and pinch to seal along the whole length. Place on the baking sheet with the seam under the roll and in the centre. Make the rest in the same way. Leave to rest for about 15 minutes before baking.

Bake for about 15 minutes. The rolls should be golden brown. Cool slightly on a wire rack. They are at their best eaten warm.

Two ways of eating rusks. Leon is tucking into them with a topping of strawberries, top, and below is the Dutch perennial, offered after the birth of a child, of beschuit met muisjes *– with little aniseed dragées, which are described on page 63.*

Chapter Three

RUSKS
Beschuit

In the seventeenth century, life in the villages of Wormer and Jisp, in the Zaan region just north of Amsterdam, revolved around rusks. Wormer alone had more than 150 rusk bakeries and was the centre of the Dutch rusk industry.[1] The bell in the tower nicknamed 'the rusk-bakers' tower' would ring early in the morning to signal the start of the day's baking and would peal a warning at six in the evening for the ovens to be put out, a necessary precaution in a region where most of the houses were built of wood. Trade thrived and a fleet of 70 ships supplied not only the local market but went as far afield as the Baltic.[2] Sometimes Wormer rusks would even find themselves on the other side of the world: packed in kegs the rusks would keep for a long time and that made them a welcome supplement to shipboard diet. But they should not be confused with *scheepsbeschuit*, their almost-namesake.

Scheepsbeschuit was also made in large quantities for ocean-going vessels, especially the whalers and herring fleets which had their home-ports here, but this hard, thin ship's biscuit was a staple and bore little resemblance to the light and crisp rusk that has always remained a treat. *Scheepsbeschuit* was made from a very basic dough, primarily flour, water and salt. If, as was sometimes the case, a little sugar and yeast were added, the biscuits were dried out after baking. This variant was, and still is, known as 'hardbread' in some coastal areas.[3] Seventeenth-century vessels usually carried both ship's biscuit and rusks.[4] They were stored in special holds which were completely lined with tin or thin sheets of lead, a process which was patented in 1664.[5] The biscuit was eaten in its natural state instead of bread, or it might be softened in water and pounded with oil and vinegar, a dish known as *propsmolder*.[6] The biscuit kept so well – if you discounted the odd worm or weevil that the sailors were careful to shake out before biting – that surplus from one voyage might be stowed away and used for a following one.[7] But *Scheepsbeschuit* usually lacked the crucial characteristic of regular *beschuit* because it was generally baked only once. The name *beschuit* is a Dutch corruption of the French word *biscuit*, 'twice cooked', an apt description as rusks are first baked, then dried out the oven. However, the alternative name *tweebak*, the Dutch translation of the word, was still popular well into the twentieth century, particularly in rural areas.

Wormer rusks received a telling accolade from the Amsterdam physician Stephanus Blankaart (1683). What apparently pleased him most was their wholesomeness, arising from an absence of sweat in the dough.[8] The near-monopoly position of Wormer was challenged in the eighteenth century, and production gradually slowed to a halt. Not only was there a decline in shipping activity, but more bread-bakers started making good rusks.[9] There was no need to go to a weekly rusk market if you could get what you wanted locally.

Initially, rusks were quite compact in structure and texture. The author of *De Verstandige Huys-houder* (The Sensible Housekeeper, 1661), having announced in the recipe title that the *'twee-back'* recipe he is giving is suitable for use on land, aboard ship and in foreign parts, hastens to add that what follows is certainly not the common 'ships' bread' version eaten by sailors and others aboard ship. It certainly sounds like a tasty product in spite of its lack of leaven. Fine rye or wheat flour is mixed with pulverized aniseed, fennel, mace and, intriguingly for the time, tamarind. Butter and honey or sugar are added, and the dough is baked as a round loaf or in whatever shape the cook chooses. It is then split and dried out in the oven.[10] In *De Ervarene en Verstandige Hollandsche Huys-houdster* (The Experienced and Sensible Dutch Housekeeper, 1720), an almost identical recipe is given, but the dough is shaped into small rolls.[11] Later, by the middle of the eighteenth century, rusks appear in more refined forms, baked in rectangular tins or paper cases and daintily sliced before being dried in the oven. By this time recipes are calling for sugar to be whisked with several eggs which is sure to have lightened the texture;[12] and yeast, too, is used in some cases.[13] These richer, *biscotti*-type rusks are no longer made on an identifiable scale in Holland; Italian *biscotti* are now a trendy product and these older rusks, which lend themselves so admirably to home-preparation, have been forgotten. But they continue to exist in places like South Africa, taken there by early colonists, and still feature prominently in local home-baking.

The early commercial rusks were made from flat rolls of featherlight, sweetish dough which were baked, split horizontally, then put back in the oven to dry to their characteristic crispness. This is not the hard crispness of melba toast or *biscottes*, it is an indescribably light and airy crispness that shatters into millions of fragments as your teeth sink into the almost weightless disc. These free-form rusks were undoubtedly delicious but they had the drawback that the domed and risen top half would wobble about on a plate, resisting all attempts to a get at it with the butter knife. Imagine the mealtime squabbles as everyone reached for a flat bottom half! But how to make two flat rusks from one roll without the wastage of trimming away much of the domed top? Amazingly simple, of course, especially with the benefit of a little hindsight: bake the roll in a metal ring with a detachable lid which would constrain the dough from rising into a dome. The baker could lift up this loose lid to check on the rising process, but this was about the only advantage. What a disaster if that day's rusk dough proved to be so unruly that it lifted the lid off of its own accord! Even the well-placed ventilation holes near the top of the ring, and in the lid itself, could not always prevent this. So the lid was eventually attached to the ring, the whole thing became a cover and this problem was solved. The ventilation holes now served a secondary but equally important purpose: you could see how the dough was rising without having to expose it to air. Draught is the sworn enemy of the light and delicate rusk dough and even the slightest suspicion of cool air could have ruinous consequences.

Though the trend was almost exclusively towards flat rusks, the free-form rusk did not disappear and, up to today, *spouwers* (*spouwen* = to split) are baked in some parts of North Holland, usually at fairtime. These rusks are flavoured with aniseed and are baked without covers. They are usually dried as a whole roll and are split at the table.

Baking rusks under covers was well established by the second half of the nineteenth century. The rusks varied in size from baker to baker, mainly because most of them had the local blacksmith make their covers.[14] They were usually round and the majority had straight sides, though some bakers preferred fluted covers. In rare cases square covers were used and sometimes a baker might use some of his rusk dough to make tea rusks. These were baked in a loaf tin with straight sides and a lid, like the tin called a Pullman nowadays. The baked loaf was sliced, cut into fingers and sprinkled with sugar and cinnamon or aniseed before it was put back into the oven. These were even more of a luxury than the ordinary kind of rusk and they would generally be eaten as a snack, accompanied by a cup of tea, instead of forming part of a meal. Aniseed rusks are a memory but cinnamon rusks are still made today, and you will find them in the shops with the biscuits, never with the other, humbler rusks.

I can use the word 'humble' now without causing any raised eyebrows, because rusks have become an everyday affair, an affordable treat. There

The equipment necessary to make rusks: the metal covers that keep them flat-topped in the manner of a Pullman loaf tin (there are regional preferences as to shape); the wooden slicing block that is used to cut them neatly in two.

was a time when they would be eaten on special occasions and average families would have them only on Sundays, if at all. Servants in past times would look forward to this crisp ending to their Sunday meal, a delicious break from the prevailing monotony. So prized were they that some people used them as a sandwich topping on rye or white bread, or even a combination of the two. White bread with butter and a rusk would have been the ultimate treat for ordinary folk.

Rusks are very time-consuming to make and most bakers had one or two 'rusk days' when they would making nothing but. Of course, those were the days when people didn't kick up a great fuss if the bread was a day old, so the baker could devote his undivided attention to his rusks. The time and work involved had to be earned, so they remained a luxury.

Things began to change around the 1870s as rusk production became more mechanized. The baker lost ground to the factories and rusks started to come within the reach of more people. But there is another factor that played an extremely important role in the development and continuity of rusks as a national food. No modern marketing plan or advertising strategy could have had more impact on the rusk industry than the coupling of rusks with *muisjes*, translated literally as 'mice', or more appetizingly, 'aniseed dragées'. The aniseed stalk protrudes slightly from the sugar coating, and that, combined with the natural shape of the seed, makes the dragée look like a minute mouse. This terminology has had many people convinced that the Dutch eat rodents as a special treat!

Towards the end of the nineteenth century, a young entrepreneur started manufacturing these dragées in large quantities. Before that, aniseed had always been prized for its stomach-soothing qualities as well as its tendency to reduce postnatal cramps. New mothers would be given gruels, porridges and breads containing aniseed. The many visitors to their bedsides would most often be given a slice of white bread, liberally buttered and sprinkled with sugar, commonly referred to as a *suikerstik*. There was nothing novel about the dragées themselves – they had been popular for hundreds of years as a flavourful aid to digestion at the end of a meal. In the late Middle Ages sugar-coated aniseed and caraway seeds known as *trigi* or *tragi* were sprinkled over dishes and used to decorate cakes and pastries.[15] Later, in the eighteenth century, they were often used to treat the siblings of a new-born baby, in the hope that this would dispose them favourably towards the latest arrival.[16] It had traditionally been a great luxury, produced in small batches by specialized pastrycooks. It was a tedious operation, requiring much stirring and rubbing to rid the seeds of the 'tails', as well as to provide the thirteen or fourteen coatings of sugar.[17] But this young manufacturer gave a new twist to an old idea and managed to get his product accepted very quickly. Perhaps the fact that he presented orange-coloured dragées to the royal family when the crown princess of the House of Orange was born, amidst a wave of publicity, gave him a hefty shove in the right direction. His heirs have a thriving business as *beschuit met muisjes* have become a permanent fixture at births. All over the country, with the possible exception of the region of Twente where they have their special *kraamschudderswegge* fruit bread, large quantities of rusks with mice are eaten whenever a baby is born. In Holland most women prefer to have their babies at home. There are excellent facilities, including postnatal homecare: qualified maternity help for ten days following the birth of a baby is quite matter-of-course. Nurse, nanny or help's responsibilities include preparing huge quantities of *beschuit met muisjes*; not only do the waves of visitors have to be catered for, but the proud father and siblings all take trays-full to treat colleagues and classmates. You won't catch the maternity help shaking the box of mice over an endless expanse of rusks, with more falling off than sticking to the butter. Her way is much more efficient: you pour the contents of the box onto a large plate, you butter the rusks liberally, then you press the buttered side of the rusks into the mice. No mess at all, and done in a flash! It says a lot for these two specialities that this treat never palls. I have never known anyone, even the most fervent dieter, refuse it. The eaters, even those who haven't received cards, know the gender of the child without having to be told. While in the early days smooth mice were used for girls and rough ones for boys, now boys get blue and white mice and girls pink and white, although some parents feel compelled to take a private stand against discrimination and their choice of colour can leave you very puzzled.

The mechanization of rusk manufacture has predictably led to uniformity. A rusk is now 8–9 centimetres in diameter and about 1.5 centimetres high. There is also a factory-produced version of the slightly larger Twents rusk which is a pale shadow of the rusks still made there by many bakers. Twente is the district around Enschede, in the north-east of the country. Some bakers have made it their speciality and they produce large quantities to supply colleagues as well. The artisan-made Twents rusk is larger, sweeter and more crisply yielding than any other rusk. I fell for them in a big way when I was introduced to them twenty years ago. We always look forward to visits from my husband's aunt, Tante Giene, who lives in Twente. Eyes aglint with greedy anticipation follow her progress as she unpacks several rolls of fresh Twents rusks from her bags which the whole family proceeds to devour with shaming eagerness and rapidity.

The Twents rusk has held its own but many other regional variants have undeservedly been condemned to obscurity. The Frisian rusk, now made by a handful of bakers in Friesland, is as large as the Twents, 11 or 12 centimetres in diameter and often fluted. Until the Second World War, a rusk known as a Frisian rusk was baked in Brabant, but it was free-form, baked without a cover. The Holland rusk was smaller and contained no glucose syrup, making it harder than most other types. The Hague rusk was similar, with a slightly sweeter taste. The Zeeland rusk-covers were almost twice as high as the others, producing something much thicker than usual. Rye flour was used in a few cases and there even used to be a free-form rye version.

Rusk-making has always been a specialist task. Bakers develop their own jealously-guarded 'secret' recipes upon which reputations are built. A rusk from a good baker is infinitely superior to a factory-made one, but very few bother to cross swords with the factories, more's the pity. A rusk recipe must be as near perfect as possible. The ingredients must be harmoniously balanced: too much or too little of a particular ingredient can have alarming consequences. Good flour is the basis. High-gluten flour gives the best result, but if the gluten content is too high it won't get a chance to develop properly and the baked dough will shrink into ugly wrinkles. Milk is the preferred liquid, although in the days when bakers didn't buy everything from wholesalers, diluted colostrum[18] was often used in rural areas in springtime. A large measure of yeast is necessary because the dough is so rich and eggs contribute to the lightness. Duck eggs used to be thought better than hens' eggs. Not only were they cheap and plentiful in the days prior to large-scale land reclamation, they are larger and the yolks have a higher fat content than hens' eggs.[19] Nowadays everything is weighed to the last milligramme and eggs come pasteurized in cartons. And where would one find a reliable supply of duck eggs in the face of intensive chicken farming? Sugar and glucose syrup are used in varying proportions and while salt is necessary to stabilize the gluten, it has an adverse effect on the crispness. The mystery ingredient is a composition known as 'rusk sweetener' or 'rusk jelly'. This is a combination of mundane things like sugar, glucose, fat and water together with more exotic potash and mind-boggling Marseille soap (Marseilles was once a principal European centre of soap manufacture, the preferred fat in their soaps being olive oil, as it was in Castile soap; its use in rusks was as a primitive emulsifier)[20] – and I even saw wood glue in one early twentieth-century manuscript recipe.[21] Bizarre though it may sound, a judicious amount of the now-forbidden Marseille soap has a beneficial stabilizing effect on the rusk dough.[22] Nowadays packages list an anonymous emulsifier, often in combination with rusk jelly, a chemical cocktail or lecithin having apparently been deemed more suitable for human consumption.

Rusk dough is kneaded very thoroughly and for much longer than bread dough. It is given a bulk rise, then divided into pieces weighing about 30 grams. After a short pause to relax the dough these pieces are rounded then flattened and placed on a baking sheet. They are covered and left to rise before being baked for 8–10 minutes in a 260°C oven. The rolls, which are now known as rusk rolls – and are sold as such in their own right – are removed from the covers and left to cool. They are split by hand or mechanically. This task requires precision or some of the finished rusks will end up being too brown or too light. The first rusk-cutters were a wooden plank-like affair with two holes for rusk rolls. A knife could be passed through the side slits to make equal halves of each roll. Now, most are untouched by human hand: machines steady and slice and flip endless batches of rolls on their way into the drying ovens. The halved rusk rolls are dried out for a few minutes at 240°C, and are packed as soon as they are cool. They must be kept very dry as the same glucose syrup which imparts such a delicate texture also attracts moisture.

Most households have an airtight cylindrical rusk container. To remove rusks from this in the Dutch way you just open the top of the wrapping and fearlessly plunge a knife into the topmost rusk. Once impaled, you tweak it effortlessly from the package. It is not the done thing to prise a rusk out with your fingers. They are closely surrounded by corrugated paper and crush easily. The knife trick is quite foolproof once you get the hang of it – my nine-year-old son is an expert. To him, as to so many other Dutch children – and not a few adults – a bread-based meal or a leisurely weekend breakfast is not quite complete without a rusk or two, topped with mice, jam or chocolate vermicelli – and in summer, a generous helping of sliced strawberries.

Rusks have culinary uses too. They are crushed to line baking tins instead of flour; they are are sometimes sprinkled on apple tart dough to absorb any excess liquid from the apples. I know many people who crumble a rusk or two into a pan of steamed chicory or Belgian endive to mop up some of the moisture that relentlessy seeps out, however well you drain it. The Dutch seldom use breadcrumbs in meatballs, substituting rusk crumbs instead, giving the meatballs their typical texture. You can even make a quick pudding, as did my mother-in-law. She would line a dish with rusks, pour puréed redcurrants over them and top this with warm custard. It never found favour with me but the rest of the family devoured it in a flash.

Chapter Four

SPICE CAKES
Kruidkoek

Cakes made with honey and spice are among the oldest known to us. Genghis Khan's army supposedly carried them as rations and they spread westwards into Europe in the packs of returning Crusaders and other travellers to the East. Centuries later, Dutch soldiers were to be issued with spice cake as rations: it was both an excellent source of energy, and kept very well.[1] They were originally an item of great luxury. Spices were so expensive that they were the exclusive preserve of the privileged classes. To begin with, sugar was also a luxury few could permit: it was treated more as a condiment than a sweetener to be added during the actual cooking process. The original spice cakes used honey as a sweetener, only gradually to be replaced in whole or in part by sugar and syrups. Honey was more readily available and perhaps more to the taste of people yet to develop a liking for sugar. However, as it became more accessible, sugar was used more often.

Several European countries have clung to the more traditional type of spice cake, with honey remaining a major ingredient. Unfortunately, as the price of honey now increases, so does the proportion of refined sugar and its derivatives. People's tastes, too, are gradually changing and we will probably never know how much this is due to bakers' and manufacturers' profit-margins rather than a genuine inclination towards another flavour. The elements are often so interwoven that, tempting though the prospect may be, it is dangerous to draw simplistic conclusions.

Holland has retained a very fine tradition in spice cakes and the fact that the Dutch East India Company once had such a firm grip on the spice trade may have helped nurture their lasting popularity. Spices had been available for centuries as caravans slowly wound their way westwards from Asia bearing their costly burdens. Once they reached the Levant and the Mediterranean, Italian traders eagerly relieved them of their goods for west European markets.[2] Spices were extremely expensive and in the late Middle Ages a pound of ginger had the same value as a sheep and a pound of saffron that of a horse. A cow could be had for the equivalent of two pounds of mace and a single pound of nutmeg commanded the same price as seven fat oxen.[3] The opening of the sea route to the East in the fifteenth and the sixteenth centuries by Portuguese navigators left that nation in control of the European spice trade in the early modern period. That is, until a Dutch innkeeper's son, Jan Huyghen van Linschoten, sought and obtained employment in Portugal. He travelled extensively in the East in Portuguese service, making copious notes and sketches which he published on his return to Holland in 1596.[4] This was a great blow to the Portuguese as his journal contained all the information that European powers needed to break Portugal's monopoly: not only navigation charts, maps, sketches and descriptions, but acute observations on the sadly diminished might of the Portuguese navy. Fired by these revelations, various European countries started clamouring for a share. The Dutch East India Company was founded in 1602 and it immediately grabbed the trade monopoly for the East Indies.[5] For almost a century terror, violence, cruelty and bloodshed produced spices in sufficient quantities to make the Amsterdam investors rich and to lower the market price, and by the time the East India Company went bankrupt in 1799, Holland and the rest of Europe had ready access to the coveted commodity.

Although generally eaten as a sweet treat, spice cakes were sometimes used in cooked medieval dishes. For carp in brown sauce,[6] for example, the sauce is flavoured and thickened with spice cake. These spice cake mixtures were generally composed in a manner that sounds uncomfortably vague to modern minds. Pepper, cloves, nutmeg and saffron weighed out in decagrams pose little problem, but interpreting 'five gingers and a *talie* of honey', even after it is converted to about five centimetres,[7] proves more challenging. To deter adulteration, local authorities sometimes laid down a spice mixture recipe by law, as was the case in Utrecht in 1432.[8] The powder (perhaps intended for sprinkling on other dishes as well as cakes) included pepper, ginger, cinnamon, nutmeg, cloves and saffron. Spice cakes of old relied heavily on pepper. It was, anyway, one of the most prized and expensive of spices – not for nothing do the Dutch use the expression *peperduur*, as expensive as pepper. Larger amounts of other spices were added over the centuries, sometimes even to the exclusion of pepper, but *peperkoek* is still used colloquially as a generic term for spice cake by many people.

Some of the cakes continue to exist in their original form. The *Deventerkoek*, a compact honey loaf flavoured with bitter orange peel, is one of the oldest existing spice cakes in Holland. Its documented history can be traced back to a city council decree from 1417, which laid out in the strictest terms how it should be made, from the quality of the ingredients to the recipe and the weight of the finished *koek*. Failure to comply brought a hefty fine of 666 guilders.[9] These rules became so legendary that much later the British poet Robert Southey confided in a letter home that only the mayor had the recipe for *Deventerkoek* and that when the baker had done his preliminary preparations the magistrate came to add a special some-thing that made the *koek* what it was.[10] The magistrate did indeed show up at the bakery, but it was to check on consistent quality rather than to add a secret ingredient. Paradoxically, the secret ingredient may well have been too mundane to dwell upon: water. Far-fetched though it may sound, Deventer water was reputedly very pure and while clean, palatable water is matter of course today, in the Middle Ages it could often prove life-threatening, unpleasant at the least. Not for nothing did recipes specify 'clean' or 'sweet' water. Around the middle of the fifteenth century, copies of Deventer's speciality began to appear, first in nearby Zwolle, then in Utrecht and Amsterdam. In Groningen, they were already great *koek*-eaters and -makers and the fact that import was prohibited of all *koeken* except *Deventerkoek* speaks for itself. And Deventer was not just trading with neighbouring provinces; much was sent abroad, especially to Scandinavia. Sales figures for 1694, a top year, show an export figure of almost 715,000 *koeken*.[11] Local lore has it that *Deventerkoek* even received celebrity endorsement, by none other than Emperor Napoleon when he passed through in 1809. It remains in a class of its own.

69

There are countless kinds of spice cake, most of which are loaf-shaped. Many are regional specialities. *Dordtse koek* from Dordrecht is fairly light in colour, as is *Groninger koek*, Groningen cake, which contains a generous amount of chopped citron. *Bossche koek*, from 's-Hertogenbosch, is ovoid with sugar nibs decorating the surface. Frisian spice cake distinguishes itself by its mixed filling, as well as by the fact that the dough isn't first left to ripen. *Texelse kleikoek*, 'clay cake' from the island of Texel, has a mouth-feel that gives it its name. *Amelandse bladjes*, Ameland 'tongues', and *Amsterdamse korstjes*, spice crusts from Amsterdam, are both small. The first is shaped as its name suggests and is similar to the *taai-taai* recipe in the *Sinterklaas* section on page 161, below. The second is very dark-coloured, but is a similar shape to the lighter and larger aniseed-flavoured Frisian *keallepoat* or *kalverpoot*, 'calf's leg'. Two rolls of dough are placed side by side and pinched together in several places for the *kalverpoot*. They spread into each other on baking and, if your imagination is good enough, you can see the shape you want. *Oudewijven* or *ollewieven koek*, a tangy, light-coloured loaf flavoured with aniseed, supposedly started out as a propitiatory offering to the spirits of the field. Usually, it has a crisscross pattern scored into the surface, but the original hand-formed version requires cubes of dough to be pressed together to make up the loaf, resulting in an irregular 'cobbled' surface when baked. Some types of cake have become extinct as they are literally redundant. The *Vollenhovense amulet*, for example, used to be cast on the waters as a talisman by fishermen sailing out on the Zuyderzee. This expanse of water has long been reclaimed and the cake is now a curiosity.

Spice cakes used to provide more than just gustatory pleasure in past centuries. All sorts of games centred around them, particularly at local fairs. *Koekhakken* (*hakken* = to chop) was one of the riskier pastimes. Special flat and chewy *koeken* would be baked for this and the participants had to use an axe to chop a straight line through two *koeken*, placed one on top of the other, in three strokes. Such sport led to innumerable accidents and various cities attempted to ban it. Amsterdam outlawed it as early as 1654,[12] but it persisted for centuries. Nowadays there is a safer version, *koekslaan* (*slaan* = to hit) which is still practised at some fairs like the Alblasserdam Horse Market held in a town between Rotterdam and Dordrecht. A *koek* is placed over a plank with a shallow central hollow slightly smaller than the *koek*. The contestant is equipped with a club rather like an angular baseball bat and has to hit the *koek* into three pieces. This is much harder than it sounds and most of the *koeken* are hit so that they fall neatly into the hollow without being parted.

The old fair custom of a *koek* lottery was less dangerous fun and it was a real treat to win the huge, beautifully gilded and glazed *koek* which often had a verse written on it. *Koeken* with verses were often given at fair-time by young men to their sweethearts. There was an intricate protocol surrounding the giving and accepting of a *koek* and many an unsuspecting boy or girl found themselves engaged to be married without meaning to be! See the comments on *Hylikmaker* in the chapter on seasonal baking on page 146 for more detail.

For the game of *koekslingeren* (*slingeren* = to swing) you needed a large open space and a long piece of *koek*. The *Deventer ellenkoek* was particularly suited to this activity. The *koek* was held with both ends in one fist and swung away from the participant. The trick was to get as large a piece as far away as possible. Competitors were usually paired against each other. Both kept the pieces that were left in their hands and the winner kept the larger pieces. The loser paid. Dice games, too, were often played with *koek* as the stake. Sometimes the stallholder charged a fixed price and the dice-thrower got as many pieces of cake as the number he threw, a gamble for both parties. It was a popular pastime during severe winters when canals and other waterways froze over and people gave themselves over to skating and sleighing. *Koek-en-zopies*, stalls selling drink and cake, appeared from nowhere, often equipped with a dice board. Before you knew it, tradespeople had migrated en masse to the ice, creating an impromptu fair with waffle and *oliekoek* stands, bakers, even coopers and cobblers, all plying their trade.[13] The term *koek-en-zopie* (which means little more than 'cake and drink') continues to exist and they spring up spontaneously along skating routes and by rinks, selling things like hot chocolate, anise milk and pea soup. *Koekhappen* (*happen* = to bite at), too, has survived the centuries. It is still popular, particularly with children, at parties and smaller scale fairs. Slices of *koek* are hung up on bits of string and a participant, blindfolded and with hands bound behind his back, is invited to eat them up just as, in England, there is much apple-bobbing at children's parties.

Enormous amounts of spice cake are eaten in Holland; fifteen million people consume 28,000,000 kilos of spice cake every year.[14] The market is also getting more and more sophisticated and, to keep their share of it, bakers and manufacturers turn out new versions with amazing regularity. Spice cakes stuffed to bursting with nuts, dried fruit and even chocolate, often made from various grain mixtures, jostle for shelf space with their more traditional brothers. It strikes me very strongly that many of the newer factory-made types seem to have an ever-increasing degree of sweetness and the pity is that the subtle taste of the dough mass is often given a firm shove into the backseat to make room for all kinds of 'modern' components. But it is not uncommon for people to go back to their old favourites after having made a determined effort to move with the times. Very little can beat the honest taste of a real spice cake and I hope it will never be

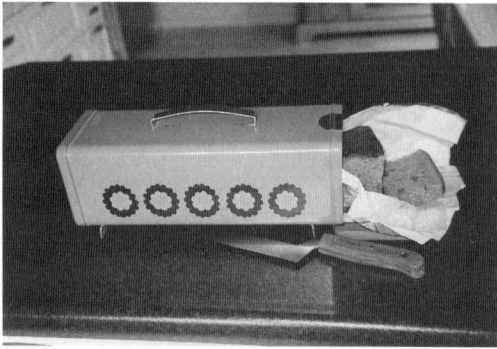

Top: a spice-cake tin dating from the 1970s (orange and dark brown with purple highlights). Middle: a collection of different spice cakes. Bottom: a cross-section of a spice cake made with chocolate and hazelnuts.

reduced to the role of 'carrier' for other ingredients. Snack-sized packages are quite a trend at the moment, as manufacturers try to corner a bit of the candy-bar market. They certainly make a healthier alternative and are popular with children as a snack for the morning break. Fitness clubs and sport canteens promote them willingly too, as their fat content is negligible.

The professional baker still makes his spice cakes in the traditional way. A basic dough is kneaded from rye flour and sweeteners and left to ripen for at least 24 hours. Centuries ago, honey used to be the only sweetener, each variety with its characteristic flavour. A baker might have a marked preference for a particular kind. Heather honey was popular and beekeepers would often take their hives to the heather-rich areas in the flowering season.[15] Some types brought agricultural benefits. Buckwheat formed an ideal target for bees and its growth was in turn heavily dependent on their cross-pollination.[16] Obviously, not all honey could be produced domestically and reinforcement was imported from places like Brittany, Chile and Mexico. Havana honey was prized for its special flavour, the result of bees gorging on sugar cane.[17] Although no longer the sole sweetening agent, many traditional recipes still require a generous addition of honey. Unrefined sugar, molasses and glucose syrups were added later, and nowadays dextrose is also used. The choice of sweetener is one of the chief factors determining the taste and texture of a spice cake.

Potassium carbonate was the first non-natural leavener. The dough had to be left to ripen for a very long time, often months, to develop enough acidity for the potassium carbonate to work properly.[18] Bicarbonate of soda is now one of the main raising agents, often a component of ready-mixed spice cake leaveners with telling names like 'Volcano'. In addition to aerating the dough, bicarbonate of soda helps to heighten the brown colour. Most spice cakes are made from rye flour and the professional baker must be able to gauge his flour accurately. One of the most important features must be its ability to absorb large amounts of liquid sweeteners properly and this will greatly influence the texture of the finished cake.[19]

After the second-stage ingredients are kneaded in, the batch of dough is shaped to fit a metal-plated wooden mould which usually measures about 50 x 100 cm. Some bakers shape the dough into individual loaves and arrange them in several snug rows within the mould, oiling their sides so that they are easy to separate afterwards. When the huge *koek* has been baked and cooled, the tough sides which came into contact with the mould itself are trimmed away and the rest is cut or divided into pieces. Frugal bakers sometimes make a simpler, cheaper dough to line the sides of the moulds. This, together with the wooden mould, protects the main batch of dough and allows it to rise slowly and evenly. The trimmings are called *kantkoek* or 'side' *koek*, and bakers will usually give them away or crumble them for use in another product. It is in fact regular practice for bakers to use *koek* crumbs from a previous batch in a new dough.

This type of spice cake is usually made by professionals. Making one loaf in a single uninsulated tin in your own domestic oven has its draw-backs and the cakes end up chewier though no less delicious. Rye is very sticky to handle and you may be tempted to stop kneading too soon, especially after the second-stage ingredients have been incorporated into the ripened dough and the going gets really tough. Not for nothing was a dough-brake used in the bakery. This iron contraption was fitted to the work-surface and its hoe-like blade was used to blend in the second-stage

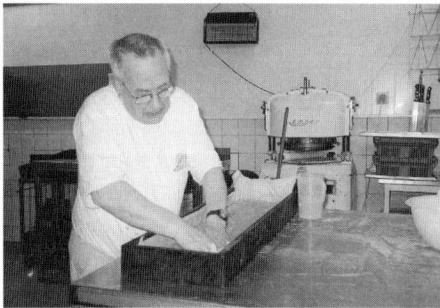

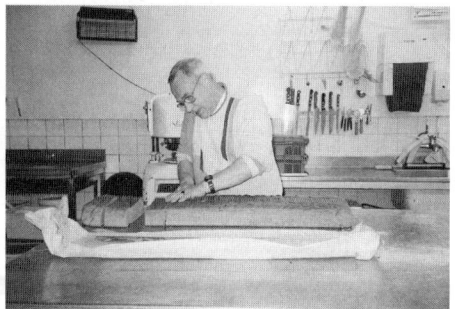

Making spice cake. From the top, left to right: kneading the dough; adding spices and raising agents; taking out a portion of the main batch; adding chocolate and hazelnuts to make a variant; flattening the dough with a moist palm once it has been put into a lined baking tray (itself made out of thick steel and wood to protect the edges of the cake from the heat of the oven); topping the hazelnut and chocolate dough with pieces of chocolate; charging the oven; slicing a cooled slab into loaves.

ingredients with a chopping movement. Some country bakers were known to knead their *taai-taai* dough with the aid of clogs,[20] their output apparently not justifying the cost of, or space for, a dough-brake. Modern bakery mixers make light work of it but most home mixers, even heavy-duty ones, will stall. Use two plastic scrapers to blend the ingredients. When they are well blended you can use your hands. All it requires is a fair amount of elbow grease. Most housewives take the easy way out and make wheaten gingerbread-type loaves. The traditional form involves more work and quite a bit of patience but the result won't disappoint you. This is one of the oldest and most typical of Dutch flavour experiences and, as you chew, it's almost as if time has stood still. Close your eyes and you might hear the clink of chainmail and the clatter of horses' hooves on the cobblestones outside – or you will with an active imagination. Let yourself be encouraged by the baker of old who hung out the following sign:

Weg met den Apotheker en Doktors vieze grillen,
Hier vind je and're pillen.
'K heb lekkere koek, zeer zoet van smaak,
Gekruit met sterk kaneel en lekker nootmuskaat.[21]

*Begone with the Apothecary and the awful whims of the
Doctor's mind,
Here you'll get lozenges of another kind,
I have delicious cake that tastes so sweet,
With strong cinnamon and delicious nutmeg, spiced a treat.*

Jacob Bussink's bakery in Deventer, established in 1593, is the longest-established spice cake maker in Holland. The original premises were burnt down in 1951, but these still have an old-world feel. This is the home of the spice cake illustrated on page 69.

BREAKFAST SPICE CAKE
Ontbijtkoek

Ontbijtkoek is often used, like *peperkoek*, to describe spice cakes in general, and literally means 'breakfast cake'. It is spice cake in its simplest form. All kinds of further enhancements like peels, preserved ginger, sugar candy, dried fruit and nuts can be added to this basic dough.

Oven: 180°C ♦ Tin: 2 l loaf tin, greased, double lined ♦ Time: about 1 hour

First stage:
600g rye flour
2 tsp ground cinnamon, 1 tsp ground ginger, $^1/_2$ tsp ground cloves,
$^1/_2$ tsp ground nutmeg, $^1/_2$ tsp ground cardamom, $^1/_4$ tsp ground mace
200g molasses
200g honey
300g water

Second stage:
100g molasses
100g honey
4 tsp bicarbonate of soda

First stage:
Sift the rye flour with the spices and set aside. Put the molasses, honey and water in a saucepan and stir over low heat until completely liquid. Cool, then pour it over the flour. Blend with two plastic scrapers then knead to a dough. Cover and set aside in a cool place for 24 hours.

Second stage:
Knead the rest of the ingredients into the ripened dough. Knead thoroughly so that there are no more white streaks or lumps and transfer to the tin. Flatten the surface with a moistened hand. Bake for about an hour. A skewer inserted into the centre should come out clean. Cool completely on a wire rack. Wrap well in clingfilm and store in an airtight container for at least 48 hours before cutting. It will have softened and become moister. Serve thinly sliced with butter.

FRISIAN SPICE CAKE
Friese Kruidkoek

This is one of the few spice cakes that does not require the dough to be left to ripen. It is more compact in texture than the previous recipe.

Oven: 180°C ♦ Tin: 2 l loaf tin, greased, double lined ♦ Time: about 1 hour

600g rye flour, sifted
1 tbsp baking powder and 1 tsp bicarbonate of soda
2 1/2 tsp ground cinnamon, 1/2 tsp ground nutmeg,
1/2 tsp ground mace, 1/2 tsp ground cardamom
300g molasses
200g light corn syrup or liquid glucose
150g soft dark brown sugar
100 ml water
50 preserved ginger, finely chopped
25g candied (bitter) orange peel, shredded or finely chopped
50g brown or white sugar candy crystals

Mix the rye flour with the baking powder, bicarbonate of soda and spices and set aside. Put the molasses, corn syrup, sugar and water in a large bowl and mix well. Add the flour mixture. Blend with two plastic scrapers then knead thoroughly, adding the other ingredients. Transfer to the tin and flatten the surface with a moistened hand. Bake for about an hour. A skewer inserted into the centre of the loaf should come out clean. Cool completely on a wire rack. Don't despair at its brick-like consistency. Wrap well in clingfilm and store in an airtight container for at least 48 hours before cutting. It will have softened and become moister, but the outer crusts will still be chewy and will resist all but the sharpest of knives. Serve in very thin slices, generously buttered.

SPICE 'CRUSTS' FROM AMSTERDAM
Amsterdamse Korstjes

These individual, deliciously chewy spice cakes are becoming quite rare as bakers hesitate to spend time on small hand-shaped articles that inevitably result in low profit margins. A great pity, because they are actually quite easy to make and could be made in large batches. They are simple and homely and so wholesome they could almost be called healthfood.

Oven: 200°C ◆ Time: about 10 minutes ◆ Yield: 12
Tin: 2 sheets, lined with non-stick baking parchment

First stage:
250g rye flour
1 ¹/₄ tsp ground cinnamon
³/₄ tsp ground ginger
³/₄ tsp ground cardamom

¹/₄ tsp ground cloves
150g honey
75 ml water

Second stage:
100g soft dark brown sugar
1 tsp bicarbonate of soda
100g honey

First stage:
Mix the rye flour with the spices and set aside. Put the honey and water in a saucepan over medium heat and stir until it is completely liquid. Cool, then pour it over the flour. Blend with two plastic scrapers then knead to a dough. Shape into a ball, cover and set aside in a cool place for 24 hours.

Second stage:
Knead the sugar and bicarbonate of soda into the ripened dough, adding the honey last. Knead thoroughly so that there are no more white streaks or lumps. Turn the dough out onto a wheat-floured surface and shape into a sausage. Cut it into 12 equal pieces. Take one piece at a time and cut it in half. Roll each of the halves into a neat cigar about 10 cm long. Place the pairs side by side on the baking sheet leaving 1 cm space between them. Leave at least 8 cm between the pairs as they will spread quite a bit while baking. Bake for about 10 minutes. They will be very soft. Leave for about five minutes on the sheet before carefully peeling away the parchment. Cool on wire racks. Store in an airtight container for 24 hours before eating. They will keep for at least a fortnight.

Chapter Five

CAKES
Taarten en Gebak

Medieval banquets were replete with sweet pies and tarts and, as there was no fixed place for them, every course might offer something sweet. While everyday meals were in general quite sober, a banquet meant overwhelming hospitality and inevitable overindulgence. Hosts enjoyed being able to present pies and tarts on a grand scale, their costliness underlining one's wealth and consequence. Ingredients were a mixture of the familiar like dried fruit, almonds, apples, curds and cream, together with the less familiar, some of which most of us would approach with the utmost reluctance. A filling made with pickled cabbage, even if left to soak in water for twenty-four hours and cooked in a sugar syrup, is not something I would enjoy myself, nor would I attempt a spinach or a chervil variant, even if it does have sugar, currants, cinnamon and candied citron. Having said that, the Provençal *tarte de blettes* (spinach beet), flavoured with sugar and nutmeg, is still a popular traditional dish. Apple tart with mashed fennel sounds quite appetizing, if a little different, and quince tart holds initial promise – quinces, spices, sugar, dried fruit, eggs, butter, almonds and pine nuts – but the addition of bone marrow does tend to make its appeal pall slightly.[1] Surely a question of conditioning, though, as people today ingest all kinds of unknown animal fats in commercially produced cakes and biscuits, seldom pausing in mid-bite to question the recipe. Bone marrow survived the centuries in Dutch Jewish cooking and a cookery book from 1956 gives a recipe for marrow tart,[2] its combination of ground almonds and marrow redolent of medieval cooking. This is partly a question of taste, but more to do with compliance with Kashrut laws; using marrow or animal fat, or pure non-dairy vegetable

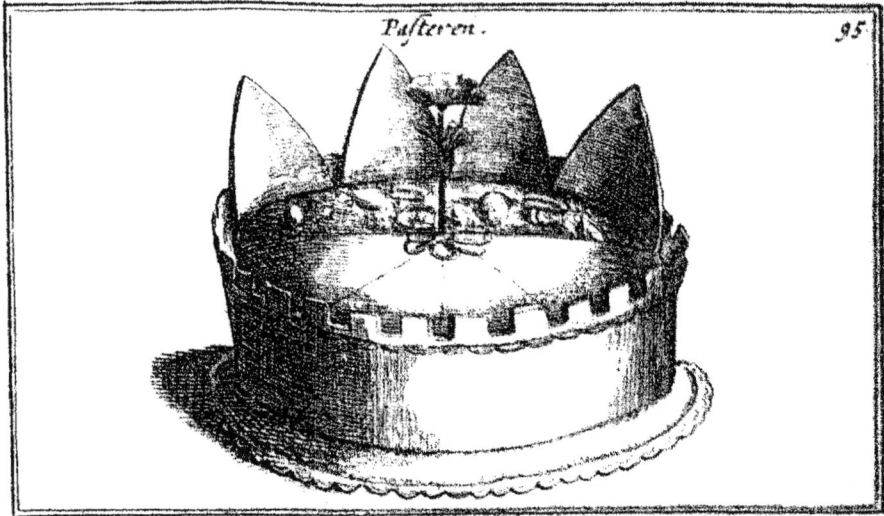

Pasteren. 95

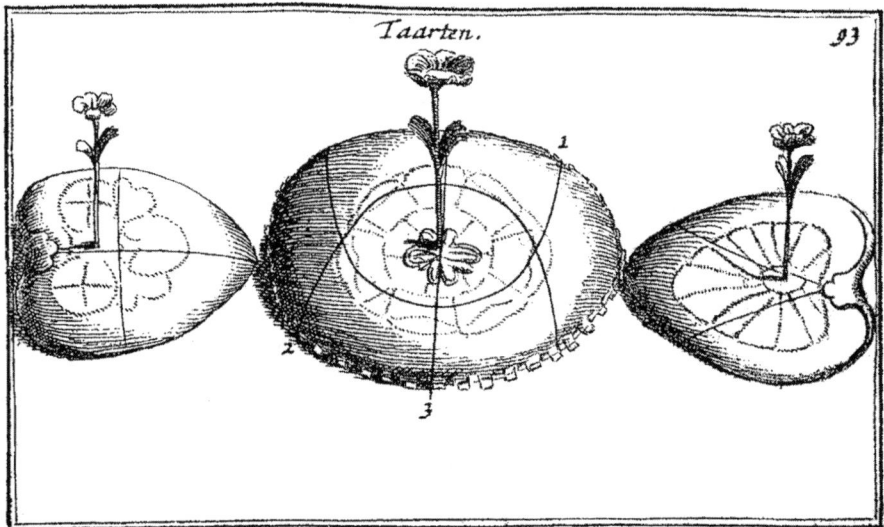

Taarten. 93

shortening, makes it possible to eat such a concoction with or shortly after a meal containing meat. Note, however, that the recipe has completely disappeared from the revised (1996) edition of this book.[3] The thought of fish oil, or half a pound of cod's liver,[4] in a cake does fill one with understandable queasiness which not even the anticipation of the accompanying almonds, sugar, saffron, ginger and rose-water completely alleviates. Nor, indeed, the reflection that the medieval hand was so heavy with spices that it was unlikely that the fishy flavour would have intruded. Using fish products was, like almond milk instead of dairy milk, a clever way of coping with ecclesiastic restrictions on the use of animal products during Lent and other times of abstinence.

Whatever we might now think of their flavour, the pies, tarts and cakes of old were culinary masterpieces and works of art in their own way, certainly according to prevailing notions. Sweet and savoury dishes alike were often given the added attraction of colour. Modern westerners sometimes regard the garishly coloured cakes and confections from distant continents with a mixture of bewilderment, disapproval and self-righteous smugness. What would they have made of their ancestors' profligate use – when they could afford it – of a wide array of 'food' colourings? Yellow was made from saffron, or even wheat grains; and saffron could be mixed with egg yolk to make gilding. Various herbs provided a green tint and lichens yielded litmus which could make a dish blue or reddish, depending on the acidity. Indigo may also have been used to make blue, and powdered sanders gave a red hue as did holly berries. Slightly more sinister, but no doubt quite effective, was producing black from blood cooked with breadcrumbs.[5]

Cakes and pies often formed eye-catching centrepieces. *De Cierlijcke Voorsnijdinghe Aller Tafel Gerechten* (The Decorative Cutting of all Table Dishes), published in 1664, gives several illustrated examples (see opposite) of the neatest and most appetizingly artistic way to cut and serve several items, including cakes and pies.[6] Some are a bit over-imaginative, like the round cake which is cut into eight pieces by first cutting two intersecting semi-circles and then dividing them with a straight line running through the centre. Others are more practical: a pie could be made more aesthetically appealing by cutting the top into wedge-shaped segments, leaving the crust attached along the outer edge so that the resulting triangular pieces of pastry could be lifted up to make a crown with the filling exposed in the middle.

I have already touched on the use of honey and its gradual replacement by sugar in the earlier chapter on spice cakes. The modern cake, however, is dependent on sugar. In the sixteenth century, cane sugar had been reaching Holland in sufficient quantities to pamper the sweet tooth of the wealthy and, by the Golden Age, its consumption had risen to almost epidemic proportions. This was reviled by straight-thinking, sober-minded clerics, one of whom bitterly reproached the moral laxity of a population so bent on the enjoyment of food that, were it not for shame, they might go so far as to send bakers and cooks to a special academy to learn their trade even better.[7] But sugar imports continued to increase as a result of much greater production and firm trade ties with Brazil and the West Indies. It came in raw liquid form and was processed in Holland. By 1660 Amsterdam boasted more than 50 sugar refineries, as many as the rest of Europe put together.[8] Not all was intended for home consumption and much was re-exported. The punishing taxes imposed on this luxurious commodity meant that even in the face of plenty, it still remained out of reach of the less well-off and remained the status symbol it long had been. Beet sugar was virtually unknown and it was not until the late eighteenth century that a production process was developed in Germany. However, when Napoleon laid an embargo on trade with England and the West Indies, beet sugar began to gain popularity as a surrogate. By the time he was defeated, supply had reached the stage where it would provide formidable competition for the reinstated cane sugar. Even so, sugar still retained its aura of luxury and, whether this was reinforced by fire-and-brimstone sermons or by a lightness of pocket, cakes and pastries were more of a treat than an everyday occurrence for many. City dwellers had readier access to cakes, pastries and sweet breads as there was an abundance of bakeries and pastry-shops. Country bakers kept things plainer – their customers being less sophisticated – so that even by the time sugar had become relatively cheap, at the end of the nineteenth century, the consumption of cakes had increased but not necessarily proportionately.

As the centuries passed, cakes began to lose more and more of their compactness. Pastrycooks and home cooks had had to rely primarily on primitive forms of yeast or the vigorous beating of eggs (very effective if properly done) to lighten their cakes, as well as leaveners like potash. Yeast had in fact never been particularly desirable in lighter preparations like cakes. In the preface to his 1752 pastry manual, master *pâtissier* Gerrit van den Brenk of Amsterdam advises against the use of yeast in cakes as it coarsens the texture and causes discoloration in almonds. Potash too, widely used in the more robust spice cakes, was to be avoided for more delicate items as it also caused discoloration. Here I must digress slightly to tell you about Gerrit and his book. This manual is in all probability the first Dutch book written specifically about the arts of cake- and pastry-making and confectionery. Gerrit van den Brenk is a baker's baker and a daydreamer's treasure. Which researcher has never wished to be able to see for himself the time and customs he or she is exploring at one remove? I know I have often indulged in futile daydreams of how lovely it would be to have the tiniest glimpse over the shoulders of bakers of old. Gerrit van den Brenk gave me my chance. As soon as I opened the fragile book and saw that he had signed the title page, the centuries receded and I felt I was being addressed personally. The book is written in a form not uncommon in Dutch household and recipe books of the time: a dialogue, in this instance, between Gerrit and an unnamed lady to whom he is divulging his recipes and tips. She presumably stands for all the ladies he would like to address. It is clear from the start that Gerrit is very passionate about his craft and is more than willing to share his knowledge and experience. So much so, in fact, that she is repeatedly obliged to call him back to the point and she often impatiently brushes aside his lengthy outpourings, telling him to get on with it. I found myself getting quite cross with her for curtailing the dialogue just as it started to get really deep and interesting, but Gerrit takes it all in perfectly good grace and tries not to let his tongue run away with him too much. By the end of the book the reader has learned a number of excellent recipes and all kinds of information about ovens, temperatures, ingredients and equipment, absorbed from Gerrit's chatty way of writing.

T'ZAAMENSPRAAKEN

TUSSCHEN EEN

M E V R O U W,

BANKET-BAKKER

E N

CONFITURIER,

Over het *Bereiden*, *Gereed Maaken* en *Bakken* van allerleye TAARTEN, GEBAK en BANKET, onder de *Pan* en in den *Ooven*. VLADENS, COMPOT-TEN, GELEYEN, PASZEN, enz.

Naauwkeurige Verhandeling over het BESLAG en het BEWERKEN van het zelven.

Het Maaken van allerleye ZUIKER PAN-WERK.

Wiskonftige Proeven en *Onderrigtingen* wegens de Hette van het tot alles noodige VUER.

Confyten van allerleye VRUGTEN en *hoe die te bewaaren.*

Het Kooken en Klaaren. van de ZUIKER en het *gereed Maaken* van al wat daar van tot Taafels of Deszerts gebruikt word.

Alles, door een geduerige *Oeffening en Onderninding*, *Wiskonftig* goed gevonden en, ter vermyding van alle onnoodige of vergeefsze Kosten, ten dienst der *Mevrouwen*, welke hunne *Liefhebberye* daar in vinden, *In het Ligt gebragt door*

GERRIT van den BRENK,

Banket-Bakker en *Confiturier* tot *Amfterdam.* Nooit voor deezen Gedrukt.

t'Amfterdam, gedrukt by de Wed: J. van EGMONT: Op de Reguliers Breê-Straat, 1752.

To get back to the subject of raising agents: the principal of the Hague Cookery School, Miss A.C. Manden published a cookery book in 1895 which was apparently so popular that it had gone into its tenth edition by 1899. She reflects on the ready availability of proprietary brands of leaveners and counsels caution as one can never be quite sure that they are completely safe.[9] One soon gathers that her preference is for natural methods like whisking eggs or relatively innocuous substances like bicarbonate of soda. Hartshorn is at this time still widely used, but the unpleasant aftertaste impels her to reject it as a suitable raising agent for cakes.

The twentieth century saw many new flavours and materials adopted by bakers and cake-makers. But there were also moments when familiar materials were no longer available, or even had to be created out of ersatz approximations. As the Second World War progressed and foodstuffs became scarcer, there were the obvious repercussions in the bakery. In a bakers' manual by H.W. Kooning published in 1942,[10] the author devotes a chapter to making do in times of crisis. He laments the fact that the war has forced bakers to use substitutes and surrogate products but manfully accepts this fate as being preferable to not baking at all. While pointing out that the taste will obviously be inferior, he comforts the baker with the thought that the customer must of necessity be less critical also. Some items rely on surpluses from times of plenty, like the melon which is made into 'candied ginger' by treating it with left-over ginger syrup. Other measures are more desperate. Among the ingredients he recommends for the cake- and pastry-baker's crisis pantry are potatoes, pulses, barley, oats, semolina, rice, peanuts and apricot kernels as well as chestnuts and artificial sweetener. What leaps out from these pages is the ardent desire to find an acceptable substitute for almonds, and almond paste in particular, Dutch bakery mainstays. Ground oatmeal can replace ground almonds in a batter but the beloved almond paste requires more attention. Mashed potato, semolina, rice, barley or chestnuts can be used with a little almond essence, or white navy beans, peanuts and apricot kernels which get closer to the texture of almonds. Up to today, beans and apricot kernels (which have a penetrating almond-like flavour) are used in inferior brands of 'almond' paste. The use of chestnuts here, as an artificially-flavoured substitute for almonds, is significant. Chestnuts, traditionally considered a last-resort ingredient, have never been valued by Dutch bakers – unlike, for example, their Austrian and French counterparts. Some people appear to have appreciated them to a degree, however, and there is a recipe from the middle of the eighteenth century that instructs us to mix two pounds[11] of cooked, finely ground chestnuts with a pound of butter and eight ounces of milk as well as a further eight ounces of curdled milk (presumably the solids), one pound of young full-fat cheese, half a pound of mature cheese, one pound of sugar, six egg yolks, and generous amounts of cinnamon and pepper. This is baked in a pastry case, then dusted with cinnamon and sugar and sprinkled with rose-water before being served.[12] From the sound of the recipe, it seems unlikely that the flavour of chestnuts would have over-ridden the taste of the other ingredients. To revert to wartime shortages: one might have expected chestnut flour to be recommended as flour of all kinds was chronically short. However, this was only the third year of conflict, so presumably morale had not yet plunged to its lowest point. Towards the end it might have been another story, when all over the country people were reduced to cooking, baking and eating dishes made with tulip bulbs.

Dutch cakes vary from the substantial, satisfying, buttery shortcakes and *appeltaart* to the light-as-air cream cakes that are a national passion. The category also includes the host of spice cakes and flans dealt with in separate chapters. The word 'cake' has been borrowed by the Dutch and is used to describe what could roughly be called pound and sand cakes. These are usually baked in loaf tins or in *gugelhupf*-like tins called a *tulband*, 'turban', in Holland. The cakes themselves are distinguished by their butteriness and the addition of flavours like broken bitter-almond maca-roons, sour cherries and spices. Three other Dutch words are used to describe what the word cake does in English. The choice of word makes its nuance clear to the Dutch listener or reader. *Koek* is an old-fashioned word which generally applies to things like spice loaves and butter doughs. *Gebak* can describe any sweet baked goods but, in its diminutive form *gebakje*, it always conjures up a picture of something both delicious and aesthetically pleasing. *Taart* is used for tarts, but even more for fancy cakes with fillings. Layer cakes are characterized by lightness and fillings include the egg liqueur *advocaat* and a popular pastry cream made by mixing a custard base with whipped cream. This can be flavoured in a number of ways and one of the most delicious is the *chipolataart* filling with maras-chino liqueur and finely chopped, steeped fruit. Nut meringues are very popular, like *hazelnoottaart* which combines hazelnut meringue layers with coffee buttercream and chopped hazelnuts. *Progrestaart* is an almond meringue sandwiched with cream. Smaller cakes include the tiny marzi-pan-covered layer cakes with their ends dipped in chocolate, rejoicing in the name *mergpijpjes* (marrowbones), a throwback to the pre-war version of a cream-filled roll of marzipan. Small pastries are often filled with almond paste or fruit. Stewed apples are baked in small rings lined with buttery pastry to produce *appelrondos* and there is also an almond-paste version. Apricot Girls are halved apricots baked on a bed of frangipan-topped pastry. Choux confections are very popular, with the huge chocolate-coated cream bun, the *Bosschebol* (native to 's-Hertogenbosch) at the front by several lengths. Another very Dutch choux bun is the banana

éclair, baked in a curved shape and filled with pastry cream and sliced banana. There is astounding choice in this field, which has been expanding ever since the post-war boom. You can buy them everywhere, at prices to suit all pockets.

Cake-eating is very much a homely pastime, something done in familiar surroundings. You buy your cakes and take them away. Sidewalk cafés offer only a limited selection and there is no proliferation of the German and Austrian type *Konditoreien*. Those that there are, are mainly seasonal and situated in tourist areas or, fittingly enough, in border towns just short of the German frontier. There actually isn't even a specific Dutch word to describe such a place and 'lunchroom', 'tearoom' or the German *Konditorei* are generally used. Whatever you do, don't step into a building that advertises itself, in English, as a 'coffee shop', as the only cakes you will get are likely to give you more pleasure than you bargained for. This euphemism applies to shops which sell legal soft drugs. A 'coffee house' or *koffiehuis*, on the other hand, is quite innocuous but even here you won't get your favourite Dutch specialities. These coffee houses are often Turkish or Moroccan, catering for the immigrant community.

Koffievisite, literally 'coffee visit', is still the most popular way of entertaining in Holland and it can mean anything from a chat with a neighbour over a mid-morning cup of coffee to a full-scale gathering of family and friends, when the coffee and cakes will usually be supplemented by a variety of salads and sandwiches. Apart from birthdays (which you can read about in detail in the chapter on seasonal baking), Sunday mornings are a favourite time for coffee visits. Most people make it a habit to keep this time for socializing. As you watch cars swish by, you can see the telltale signs like the bunches of flowers for the hostess in the rear window. In closely knit communities, it is quite customary for adult children and their families to meet at a mother's or mother-in-law's house, often after church, where they can discuss the week's news and exchange gossip over coffee and cakes. On weekdays you will see bakers' delivery vans stop and disgorge several huge boxes at various business premises. Birthdays, even if they fall at the weekend, and special milestones – even leaving one job for another – are a time for treating colleagues to cakes. Some people will make their own, but by far the majority gratefully rely on their baker. And receptions of all sorts invariably start with coffee and a selection of cakes or *petits fours* before moving on to savouries and alcoholic beverages.

APPLE TART
Appeltaart

Appeltaart is not a pie, nor a tart, nor quite a cake. It defies definition but it ranks as the nation's favourite sweet baked article. It appears in countless versions in the kitchens of home-bakers, and every self-respecting bakery or pastry shop has its own special *appeltaart*.

As far as the apples go, I am spoilt for choice, though the tartly juicy Goudrenet (what the British call a Golden Reinette) is still the universally-acclaimed favourite *taart* apple. My family's village is located at the heart of the Betuwe, the region to the west of Nijmegen, Holland's fruit basket for centuries now. Apples and pears abound in the surrounding orchards and in the summer I can buy strawberries, raspberries, redcurrants, cherries and all kinds of other fruit fresh from the farmers, one of whom has recently taken to rearing ostriches under the trees. Come the harvest, life in the village revolves around the apples. Many local women find welcome part-time employment as pickers. As I write this, the harvest has just drawn to a close. The barns and cold-stores are full, and the farmers are happy because, in spite of the drought this summer, the quality of the apples is excellent. Today, as I cycled home with the children, I caught the unmistakable aroma of apples coming from a nearby barn, one of the pleasantly familiar village smells.

Apples have long formed the basis of Dutch sweet baked treats, as recipes from the Middle Ages will bear out. There was quite some variety in their preparation, including steps we would find quite fiddly or even superfluous. One medieval apple tart involves filling a yeasted pastry case with chopped apples, putting on a pastry lid and baking until the apples are tender. Then the top is lopped off, the apples are mashed with a profusion of ground spices and powdered sugar, then topped with softened sugar biscuits and baked until the topping has become crisp.[13] Others are simpler, requiring puréed apples to be mixed with cream and eggs and baked in a pastry case,[14] or apples stewed in sweet wine and spices then baked in a case.[15] Some are more pudding-like, using puréed apples (often first simmered in wine), butter, sugar, eggs and spices, mixed with white breadcrumbs.[16] The result was then baked, or covered and cooked over the fire in a special pan with coals heaped over the cover. This *taartepan* can be seen as the original Dutch oven, and would have been more accessible to households whose means did not permit a proper oven.[17] Another variant of this pudding-like concoction is the *schoenmaeckerstaert* or cobbler's tart, in which a very similar puréed filling is baked between two layers of breadcrumbs.[18] This is still made today, kept alive by women's magazines in a nostalgic mood, but rusk crumbs often replace the breadcrumbs. Contemporary apple tarts tend to use chopped apples, cinnamon and sugar as a filling. In the Middle Ages, too, similar tarts were made, but they were usually enriched with much butter and several egg yolks.[19] Modern tastes haven't changed that significantly, nor have we become less inclined to richness. Spices are certainly used more cautiously, but the butter and eggs from the fillings of old have migrated to the pastry, which has put its stodgy past behind it and is worth eating. This could not always have been said of its predecessors which were often simply vessels for a filling: sometimes elaborately decorated, but primarily intended as showpieces for the table rather than a tasty complement to the filling. A recipe from *Den Verstandigen Kok*, written by Amsterdam doctor P. Nyland and published in 1711, gives recipes for the more conventional apple tarts consisting of spiced apples baked in pastry cases, but one variation is more eye-catching. Apples are simmered with rice and wine to a porridge. Sugar, cinnamon or powdered sandalwood (for its colouring properties) are added along with rose-water and the mixture is pressed through a sieve and baked.[20]

The following recipe is for the most popular type of Dutch apple tart. If you top this with crumbs (from the chapter on flans on page 104), instead of the pastry ropes, it becomes *appelkruimeltaart*, apple crumb tart.

Oven: 180°C ♦ Tin: 24 cm round spring-form tin, greased and floured
Time: 60–70 minutes

Pastry:	Filling:
300g all-purpose flour	*4 large tart apples*
1 tbsp baking powder	*juice of ¹/₂ a lemon*
¹/₈ tsp salt	*75g sugar*
200g chilled butter, cubed	*50g raisins*
150g caster sugar	*50g currants*
1 egg, well beaten with 1 tbsp water	*1 ¹/₂ tsp ground cinnamon*
grated zest of ¹/₂ a lemon	*2 tbsp cornflour*

Make the pastry first. Mix the flour, baking powder and salt in a large bowl. Rub in the butter until the mixture resembles coarse breadcrumbs, then mix in the sugar. You can use a food processor up to this point. Reserve 1 tbsp of the beaten egg. Add the rest of the egg and lemon zest to the mixture and knead lightly with the fingertips to bring the pastry together in a ball. Set aside while preparing the filling.

Peel, quarter and core the apples. Slice them just under 1 cm thick. Toss well with the other filling ingredients. Press two-thirds of the pastry into the tin so that the bottom is fairly evenly covered and the sides come up to about 3 cm. Fill evenly with the apple mixture. Use the rest of the pastry to make about 12 short ropes. Press to keep the dough together – this pastry responds well to rough treatment. Make a lattice pattern with the ropes. Brush with the reserved egg and bake in a preheated oven. Reduce the heat to 160°C after 20 minutes, and bake for a further 40 to 50 minutes. Leave to cool in the tin for about 10 minutes before releasing the clip and transferring carefully to a wire rack. Serve at room temperature, or slightly warm, with sweetened whipped cream.

Apple tart: laying down the latticed top; the finished tart as it comes from the oven.

BUTTER SHORTCAKE
Boterkoek

Boterkoek is one of the simplest and purest of Dutch treats – as long as it is well made. It should be very buttery, but not so buttery that it weeps, and, ideally, the dough should be left to ripen overnight. The shallow baking tin usually referred to as a sandwich tin in most English-speaking countries is called a *boterkoekvorm* in Holland; I don't think I need say more about its popularity! Over the years I have made hundreds of them, as I ran the cake stall at the annual bring-and-buy sale at my children's school. *Boterkoek* was my best seller, made to order. Traditionally, they are most often made plain or topped with blanched almonds. Preserved ginger used to be more popular than it is now, particularly in the Jewish community. I offered them in a few other flavours as well but, villagers being villagers, the plain ones sold best. I strongly recommend my own favourite: walnut. Though by no means traditional, it has attracted many converts.

Oven: 180°C ♦ Tin: 24 cm round, greased, base-lined and floured
Time: 20–25 minutes

150g caster sugar
250g all-purpose flour
¼ tsp salt
zest of ¼ lemon
200g (unsalted) butter
1 egg yolk
a little beaten egg for glazing

One of the following flavourings (optional):
50g walnuts, finely chopped
100g preserved ginger, drained and chopped
75g dessicated coconut
50g blanched whole almonds
50g skinned hazelnuts

Mix the caster sugar, flour, salt and lemon zest together in a large bowl. Add the softened butter and the egg yolk and knead until everything is well mixed in. If you are using walnuts, ginger or coconut, knead them in now. Shape into a ball and put it in a sealed plastic bag in the fridge overnight.

Next day, remove the dough from the fridge and allow it to get to room temperature. Knead it very briefly, shape it into a ball, flatten the ball and put it in the prepared tin. Use your hand to flatten it as evenly as possible to fit the tin. Brush with beaten egg. If you are using almonds or hazelnuts press them into the top. For the other kinds, score a plaid pattern into the top with a fork. Bake into a preheated oven for about 20–25 minutes. *Boterkoek* should never be crisp or hard so it should be baked until just done. It will be soft when it comes out of the oven. Leave it to cool to lukewarm in the tin then turn it out carefully onto a wire rack to cool completely. Store in an airtight container in a cool place so that the butter doesn't go rancid. I find it at its best after 24 hours, and it will keep for at least a week. It can also be frozen for up to two months. Thaw unwrapped at room temperature. Serve in small squares.

COCOA AND CHOCOLATE

The Dutch have played a major role in the chocolate story ever since the their vessels traded outward-bound European manufactured goods with the exotic offerings of distant ports. After boldly seizing islands off Venezuela in the 1620s, the Dutch established a port on Curaçao, greatly increasing their trading presence in the Caribbean. Cacao and silver, much of it contraband, were prized cargoes. Dutch ships reputedly took cacao plants to Indonesia and Ceylon, as well as to Fernando Po and São Tomé, whence they eventually reached several other African countries including Nigeria and Ghana, the world's two largest producers today. The Dutch soon replaced the Spaniards as the most important cacao traders and by the middle of the seventeenth century chocolate had become as popular in Holland, Italy and France as it was in Spain, spreading later to the rest of Europe. By the eighteenth century, there were 27 factories in Holland which processed the beans.

The most important development came in 1828 when King Willem I granted a patent to Coenraad van Houten for an improved method of processing chocolate. Coenraad's father, Casparus van Houten, had opened a factory in Amsterdam in 1815, where chocolate was made in the manner usual at that time: the roasted beans were ground to a thick paste, sometimes sweetened with honey or sugar, then poured into moulds to make tablets. Coenraad used a wooden screw-press to extrude the cacao-butter, leaving a fatless mass that could be pulverized to cocoa as we know it. His monopoly was limited by the ten-year patent and he sold presses to other European manufacturers, including Cadbury's and Fry's. Not only was cocoa invented in this way, but the way was open to the production of an improved kind of chocolate in which cacao-butter was an important ingredient. Coenraad experimented further with a process he had heard that the

Indians used. They had added wood ash to chocolate, so van Houten treated his cocoa with potash to soften the taste and heighten the colour. This alkalizing process is known today as 'Dutching' and van Houten brand-name cocoa still graces supermarket shelves in many countries, though the company now belongs to a Swiss multinational.[21]

Over 500,000 tonnes of cacao still pass through Amsterdam each year – 20 per cent of the world's production. Much of it is processed in one way or another before it leaves the country, but quite a lot stays behind. The Dutch are great chocolate eaters, with an average of 6 kilos per person per annum.[22] But I have always been amazed – and not a little disappointed – that the modern bakery makes so little use of cocoa and chocolate. One would think that so close an historical connection would make it quite standard, but the Dutch prefer to drink their cocoa and eat their chocolate. Although there are not many cakes which use chocolate as an actual ingredient, rather than as a decorative element, those that there are, are excellent.

Older recipe books make good use of cocoa in cakes. They can some-times rival American cakes for richness and cocoa content. *Betje de Goedkoope Keukenmeid* (Betje the Cheap Kitchenmaid), which was first published in 1850, gives a recipe for a deliciously chocolate-rich cake[23] in which almost equal quantities of butter, sugar, ground almonds and cocoa are mixed with lemon rind and egg yolks, with the whisked whites added separately to make a surprisingly light affair. The finished article is glazed with melted loaf-sugar mixed with cocoa, egg-white and lemon juice whisked to fluffy lightness. Ironically, this sort of cake is now being reimported into Holland via food magazines and cookery books from the English-speaking world and people ooh and aah over their richness and deliciousness and chocolate-ness, forgetting that basic Dutch cookery books once boasted similar treasures.

CHOCOLATE-FLECKED CAKE
Bretontaart

Oven: 200°C ♦ Tin: 24 cm tin, greased, base lined and floured
Time: about 25 minutes

Cake:	Filling:
4 eggs, separated	*250 ml milk*
100g caster sugar	*75g sugar*
zest of $^1/_2$ lemon	*2 egg yolks*
100g all-purpose flour	*2 tbsp cornflour*
$^1/_8$ tsp salt	*$^1/_2$ vanilla pod, scraped*
75g semisweet chocolate,	*icing sugar for dusting*
finely chopped and	*150 ml whipping cream*
sifted to remove powder	

Topping:

300g marzipan (optional)	*50g semisweet chocolate,*
25g butter	*chopped into small pieces*

Whisk the egg yolks with 75g of the caster sugar until pale and fluffy. Add the lemon zest and set aside. In another spotlessly clean bowl, using a clean whisk, whisk the egg whites until they begin to foam. Add the 25g caster sugar and whisk until stiff peaks form. Gently fold the whites into the yolk mixture, about a third at a time. Fold in the flour sifted with the salt and the chopped chocolate. Transfer to the baking tin, level the top and bake for about 25 minutes. A skewer inserted into the middle of the cake should come out clean. Invert onto a wire rack, remove the paper and leave to cool.

Make the custard while the cake is baking. Dissolve the cornflour in 3 tablespoons of the milk in a medium-sized bowl. Whisk in the egg yolks and set aside. Put the rest of the milk with the sugar and the scrapings from the vanilla pod into a saucepan and bring to the boil, stirring to dissolve the sugar. Turn the heat down a little. Remove about one teacup of the boiled mixture and pour it over the yolk mixture, whisking continuously. Pour this mixture back into the milk and keep on whisking until it has become quite a thick custard. Do not boil once the egg yolks are added. Transfer to a bowl and dust the top lightly with icing sugar to prevent a skin forming. Set aside to cool.

When you are ready to assemble the cake, cut it horizontally into three thin layers and put the bottom layer on a serving plate. Whip the cream until soft peaks form and whisk it into the cooled custard. If you going to use marzipan, reserve 2 tablespoonsful of this custard, using the rest to sandwich the 3 layers together. If using marzipan, roll it out thinly between two sheets of clingfilm or on a worktop lightly dusted with icing sugar, to a diameter of about 35 cm. Spread the reserved filling onto the top of the cake. It won't cover the top, just make sure it is fairly evenly distributed as this is the glue that will anchor the marzipan. Cover the cake neatly with the marzipan. Pat it gently into place with a flat hand and use a pastry wheel or sharp knife to trim any excess from the edges. Put the chocolate and butter in a heatproof bowl over a pan of barely simmering water. The bowl should fit snugly over the pan and should not touch the water. Stir until the chocolate and butter have melted and are well combined. Use a large palette knife to spread this evenly on the top and sides of the cake. Keep chilled, away from strong smells, until ready to serve. Cut with a knife held under hot water, and dried quickly, to prevent the chocolate from tearing raggedly. Let the slices come to room temperature before serving.

ADVOCAAT CREAM CAKE
Advocaattaart

Domestic brands of advocaat are very thick, with a consistency halfway between custard and pudding, and some require patience to serve – a glob falling out every few seconds – so it can take some time to empty the bottle. The connoisseur's rule of thumb is the thicker the better, and nowadays added refinements have crept in like free-range egg advocaat. Advocaat, whose full name is *advocatenborrel* or lawyers' drink, is made on a similar principle to stove-top egg custard, with brandy replacing the milk. It was originally made with yolks alone and the whites were sweetened and whipped to top it. In the present day, it is topped with whipped cream as most people prefer to buy the excellent commercial product, made by large manufacturers as well as artisans, and those who make it at home generally use whole eggs. The traditional process is quite laborious: the ingredients must be heated in a bain-marie (often improvised with a large tin placed in a pan of water) and must be kept in motion to prevent them from curdling. A flat, masher-like instrument is generally used with an up-and-down movement to enable the thickening liquid to pass freely through the holes. The process is usually referred to as mashing. (See the photographs on page 97.) Lack of time need not necessarily be an insurmountable problem. Modern times have brought an alternative method. I was recently given a recipe for microwave advocaat, made in just a few minutes.

In our home district, where there are lots of apple orchards, growers sell direct from their front halls – and they will often further entice the buyer by offering home-made advocaat, lined up so handsomely on the shelf.

Eating advocaat is an occasion in itself and women who don't normally drink alcohol feel quite free to indulge. Who can blame them? Spooning it into your mouth, from the dainty advocaat glass with a conical bowl, you feel that you are eating a luscious, spiked pudding. The Dutch are very partial to advocaat, though it is considered a bit old-fashioned and womanish; even if an emancipated male friend of ours demands it by the tumblerful at birthdays. The younger generation prefers to have its advocaat in a cake filling or chocolate centre, combining the best of both worlds.

This kind of cake is eaten all year round, but advocaat enjoys a dizzy spell of fame at Easter when yellow and eggy things are in great demand. The finishing touches are usually adapted to the season. Some bakers are content to stick in chocolate chicks making a desperate bid for freedom from cracked shells. Others use a more traditional decorative pattern, piping circles of whipped cream onto the cake and filling them with advocaat to look like sliced boiled eggs or fried eggs, depending on your imagination.

Oven: 190°C ♦ Tin: 25 x 35 cm straight-sided tin, greased and floured
Time: about 15 minutes

Cake:
4 tbsp water
50g butter, cubed
25g cocoa
100g all-purpose flour
¼ tsp baking powder
⅛ tsp salt
4 eggs
125g caster sugar
1 ½ tsp vanilla extract

Filling:
500 ml whipping cream
2 tbsp sugar
150 ml chilled thick advocaat
semi-sweet chocolate shavings
to decorate (optional)

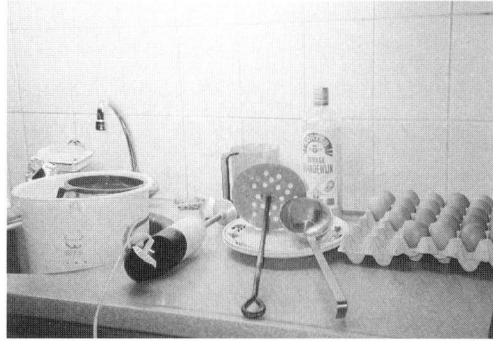

Making advocaat: the equipment, including the 'masher'; cooking the custard in a large tin placed in a bain-marie (and using the masher); ladling it into jars; the finished product. Mrs Verploeg, with the patterned apron, is a registered advocaat-maker and is permitted to use the description 'artisanal' on her labels. Her daughter Corry (in the white apron) is the maker of the apple tart illustrated on page 90.

For the cake, put the butter and water in a small saucepan and heat until the butter has melted. Leave to cool slightly. Sift the cocoa, flour, baking powder and salt together and set aside. Whisk the eggs with the caster sugar and vanilla until thick and pale. When the whisk is raised it should leave a trail. Fold in half of the flour mixture, followed by the butter. Gently fold in the rest of the flour. Transfer to the prepared tin. Level and bake for about 15 minutes or until a skewer inserted in the centre of the cake comes out clean. Invert onto a wire rack and leave to cool. Cut the cooled cake into 3 equal rectangles.

Whip the cream with the sugar until peaks hold their shape. Fold in the chilled advocaat and use to sandwich the cake layers and to cover the top and sides. Decorate with the chocolate shavings. Chill (away from strong smells) for at least 6 hours before eating. The cake layers will become more tender as the moisture from the filling seeps in. Eat within 48 hours.

Chapter Six

FLANS
Vlaaien

*V*laaien are large, flat flans made traditionally with a rich yeast dough and a sweet filling, for several centuries a speciality of the southern province of Limburg. The word appears in the Dutch language in the fourteenth century as *vlaeye*[1] and the family name Vladbecker, flan baker, can be found in early fourteenth-century parish registers in Limburg.[2] Its background is religious and flans appear in early medieval Germany in a more primitive form, as offertory bread, baked by nuns and consecrated on Easter Sunday, a connection echoed in Switzerland where Easter Sunday is sometimes called *Fladen Suntig*. In Holland, flans are now baked or bought and eaten all year round, all over the country, but there was a time when they were exclusive to Limburg, kept for special occasions like fair days, holidays both religious and secular, and weddings. Large quantities would be made and a well-filled larder might hold more than two dozen. They would be served with afternoon coffee, each one cut into eight pieces. This was a generous slice when you consider that a traditional *vlaai* tin was about 32 centimetres in diameter, but those with large appetites might eat a whole flan at one sitting.[3] It is puzzling why the flan remained virtually unknown outside Limburg for several centuries. There is no obvious answer. Subtle religious pressure, with its inevitable connotations, may have formed a kind of conditioning. In 1569, the Dutch Protestant politician and writer Marnix van St Aldegonde spiritedly attacked the Catholic church and condemned, among other things, the prominent position given to holy ashes, sanctified Easter eggs and *'vlaeyen'*.[4] If this was a prevailing opinion, it may well have contributed to keeping the flan in predominantly Catholic Limburg, out of Protestant clutches elsewhere in the country.

This flan shop advertises that its products are brought daily from Limburg.

Although bread was often made at home in Limburg, *vlaaien* were still a special treat as they were made from enriched dough. Those with no bakhouse or oven of their own would take their flans to a local baker, or to a neighbour, to be baked. It is rather ironic that now, when most modern homes have ovens, fewer flans are baked at home. Once equipped with the ingredients for the dough, the filling posed less of a problem. Home-grown fruit was traditional: fresh, bottled in syrup or dried, depending on the kind of fruit and the season. Apples are used in several ways and there is apple crumb flan, latticed apple flan, double-crust apple flan and apple sauce flan. Dessert pears as well as stewing pears are used and *oeftenvlaai*, a speciality little known beyond Limburg, uses stewed and puréed home-dried pears. The pears were usually dried whole. They were repeatedly slipped into the bread oven as it cooled after baking, their juices concentrating to produce a unique flavour. Nowadays they can simply be dried in a slow oven. Prunes, as well as fresh plums, are used and prune flan was traditionally made in the fortnight prior to Easter; Easter itself would be celebrated with a creamy white *rijstevlaai*, rice pudding flan.[5]

Flans can be the ultimate comfort food – even semolina pudding can be used as a filling. Sometimes a pudding layer is baked in a flan case and finished off with fresh fruit. Buttery dough crumbs are often baked onto a fruit topping and may even be used as the sole filling. Even humble vege-tables, from rhubarb to carrots, can also be pressed into use. You can make literally hundreds of kinds of flans, in various combinations with fruit, puddings, custard and even meringue. Anything goes. Unfortunately this notion has been greatly abused by commercially-minded flan merchants, and nowadays you will find any number with exotic-sounding names, most of which generally fail to live up to expectations. Though it's hard to know what to expect when confronted with names like Hawaii, Spanish, Irish Coffee and Peachy Passion Fruit. Fillings get lighter and airier and bavaroises and mousses are all the rage. True to the theory that swirls and swags of whipped cream improve the taste and appearance of anything, cake and pastry bottoms are often filled with fruit or mousse, slathered with whipped cream and garnished with chopped nuts and chocolate shavings, to be sold as *vlaaien*. Fortunately, though, you can still buy a whole range of traditional flans alongside the successive waves of more fashionable ones. What started out as a homely treat for special occasions has now become a mass-produced national fast-food. In the last decade or so flan shops have sprung up all over the country. No baking is done on the premises and they have the flans brought in fresh every day from large specialist bakeries in Limburg, creating the opportunity to advertise the product as the genuine Limburger article.

The best flans are still home-made. You can use fresh, tinned or bottled fruit. In Holland you can buy tins of flan filling, scaled-down versions of what some commercial bakers use, with thickener already added. Even if you use bottled or tinned fruit yourself to make your own filling, the result is usually far more appetizing than the generally mushy ready-made fillings. Eat the flans as freshly as possible, at room temperature. A moderate amount of freshly whipped cream, unswirled and unswagged, but sweetened to taste, makes an excellent accompaniment.

A bakery with a display of every sort of flan. The lattice-topped Limburger and Linzer flans tend to be sold as a whole or a half, while the newer types of luxury flans (with a mousse or bavarois filling) will often be sold by the slice.

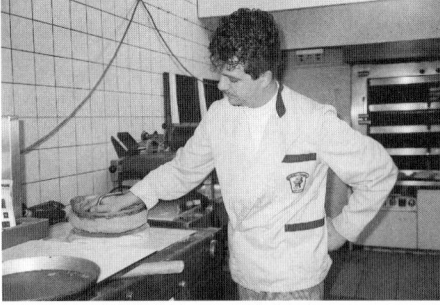

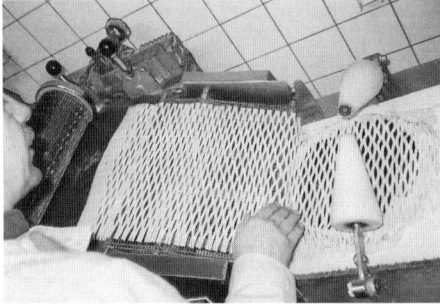

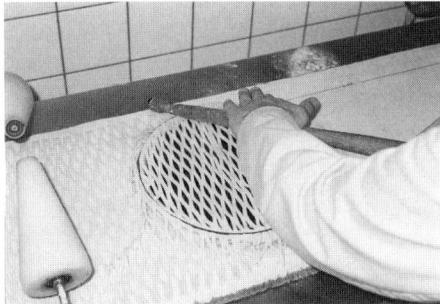

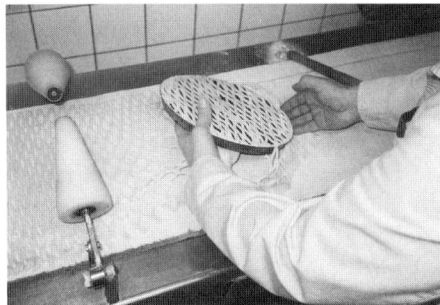

Making a Limburger flan in the bakery. The baker has a special piece of equipment to tamp the dough evenly into the tin. Once the filling has been added, his life is made the easier by the machine-rolled lattice top being quickly and effectively dispensed.

BASIC FLAN DOUGH

Single Crust Flan Dough:	Latticed Flan Dough:
175g all-purpose flour	*225g all-purpose flour*
$^3/_4$ tsp easyblend yeast	*1 tsp easyblend yeast*
15g sugar	*25g sugar*
generous $^1/_8$ tsp salt	*$^1/_4$ tsp salt*
25g butter, melted	*35g butter, melted*
$^1/_2$ egg, lightly beaten	*1 egg, beaten*
6 ml milk, warmed to 37℃	*8 ml milk, warmed to 37℃*

Mix the dry ingredients together. Add the butter, egg and milk and mix well with a spatula until the dry ingredients are well moistened. Knead well until elastic. Shape into a ball and put it in a large bowl covered with a tea towel wrung out in warm water. Put it in a warm draught-free place until doubled in volume. Knock back the risen dough and knead until once again elastic. Roll out on a floured surface to a circle about 32 centimetres in diameter. Line the sponge tin (see the apricot crumb flan recipe below) with this and trim the edges if necessary. Prick the base in several places with a fork, cover loosely with lightly-oiled clingfilm and leave to rise again. When the dough has risen visibly the flan case is ready to be filled.

PUDDING

20g cornflour
250 ml milk
1 egg yolk
50g sugar
the scrapings of $^1/_2$ a vanilla pod

In a small bowl, dissolve the cornflour in 4 tbsp of the milk. Whisk in the egg yolk and set aside. Put the rest of the milk with the sugar and vanilla scrapings in a saucepan and bring to the boil. Reduce the heat and pour a small cupful of the hot milk into the cornflour mixture, whisking as you pour. Whisk this slowly back into the milk in the saucepan. Keep on whisking until the mixture has thickened so that the whisk leaves a trail in the pudding. Scrape the pudding out into a bowl and cool. You can cover the top with clingfilm or dust it lightly with icing sugar to prevent a skin forming. Stir before using.

BUTTERY CRUMBS
Kruimels

These buttery crumbs can be used to top the filling of your choice or as a filling in their own right. In that case, remember to increase amounts.

100g all-purpose flour
50g caster sugar   *½ tsp salt*
75g butter, melted and cooled

Put the dry ingredients in a large bowl and mix well. Pour the butter over them. Use a fork to mix until all the butter has been absorbed and there is no loose flour left. Mix lightly without pressing or the lumps will be too large.

APRICOT CRUMB FLAN
Abrikozen-kruimelvlaai

This is just one of the many ways that a flan can be built up, layer by layer. A pudding base is topped with apricots, finished with buttery crumbs. You could use fresh or bottled apricots for this recipe or even make a coarse purée from the apricots, binding it with a little cornflour.

Oven: 200°C ♦ Time: 35–45 minutes
Tin: 24 cm round sandwich tin, sides at least 4 cm high, greased

1 quantity single crust flan dough
1 quantity cooled pudding
1 quantity buttery crumbs
750g fresh apricots, stoned and halved, or
500g bottled or tinned apricots (drained weight), drained and sliced
50g sugar if using fresh apricots

Make a dough case as described in the recipe for flan dough. Fill the risen dough case with the pudding. For fresh apricots, arrange them snugly on top of the pudding – they will shrink on baking – with the cut side up. Sprinkle with the sugar. For bottled or tinned apricots, arrange the slices neatly on top of the pudding. Sprinkle the crumbs evenly on top of the fruit and bake in a preheated oven for 35 to 45 minutes. Turn out onto a wire rack to cool.

RICE PUDDING FLAN
Rijstevlaai

This is one of the most unpretentious of flans which can be served as it is or with a topping of cherries and cream. It has been made in varying forms for centuries and a recipe from 1510 gives a Lenten version made with almond milk, flavoured with ginger and cinnamon.[6] In Zeeland there is a variant called *paptaart* or porridge tart with a filling of *Spaanse pap*, Spanish porridge, a distant echo of the Spanish dominance of the region.[7] It is a small custard tart which traditionally uses a generous amount of rice flour as a thickener, flavoured with cinnamon or rose-water.[8] Modern bakers seem to have opted for a cornflour pudding similar to the pudding recipe given in this chapter and have replaced the yeast dough with pastry.

Oven: 200°C ◆ Time: 40–50 minutes
Tin: 24 cm round sandwich tin, sides at least 4 cm high, greased

1 quantity single crust flan dough
700 ml milk
scrapings of ½ vanilla pod
100g round-grained pudding rice
100g sugar
3 eggs, separated
sweetened whipped cream for serving

Cherry topping (optional):
350–400g bottled or tinned cherries, in light syrup (drained weight)
100 ml of the syrup, additionally sweetened if desired
2 tsp cornflour

Make the filling first. Put the milk and vanilla scrapings in a large heavy-based saucepan and bring to the boil. Stir in the rice and bring to the boil once more. Reduce the heat, cover and let it cook over low heat for 50–60 minutes. Stir from time to time to prevent it from catching. The rice will be thick and porridge-like when it is done. Set aside to cool to lukewarm. Make the dough while the rice is cooking.

Prepare the dough as described in the basic recipe. When it is ready to be filled, whisk the yolks and 50g sugar into the rice. Whisk the whites until foaming. Add the rest of the sugar and whisk to soft peaks. Fold into the rice mixture and pour into the dough case. Bake in a preheated oven for 40–50 minutes. The top will be golden brown. Leave to cool for about 5 minutes in the tin before transferring carefully to a wire rack to cool thoroughly. Eat at room temperature. It will keep in the refrigerator for up to three days, but is best eaten as freshly as possible. Do not reheat.

For the cherry topping, dissolve the cornflour in 1 tbsp of the syrup. Put the rest of the syrup in a saucepan and bring to the boil. Reduce the heat and stir in the cornflour. Stir until the syrup has just thickened. Add the well-drained cherries and remove from the heat. Pour over the lukewarm or cold flan, spreading out evenly.

CURD CHEESE FLAN
Kwarkvlaai

The New World popularity of cheesecakes, made from the cream cheese that was the invention of two nineteenth-century American dairymen, often threatens to overshadow their ancient and distinguished lineage. Curd cheesecakes were made in ancient Rome and regularly graced the tables of the wealthy in medieval Holland. The cheese was generally made at home by various methods still in use today. Cream was boiled and soured with, for example, elder vinegar[9] or, perhaps, naturally soured milk. It would then be hung to drain in a fine cloth and used to make one of the many

Putting the finishing touches on a luxury flan (left) where a blind-baked sweet pastry case has been filled with a mousse or bavarois and is then more or less elaborately decorated. On the right is a Linzer flan which also has a pastry base, but with the traditional lattice top like the yeast-risen Limburger flan.

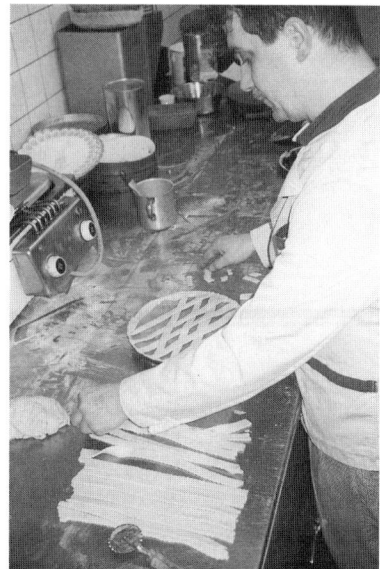

Another view of the Linzer flan, top. Below, the rack fills up with many different sorts of flans, the achievement of a morning's work.

cheesecakes, most of which were sweet. Some were very simple, just curds, yolks, butter and flour baked in pastry.[10] Presumably a little sugar, a popular condiment, would have been sprinkled on it before serving. A cookery book from 1510 gives a recipe for *bruyn taerte*, brown tart, in which curd cheese is combined with sugar and spices like cloves, nutmeg, mace, cardamom and ginger, giving the colour of its name.[11] A manuscript from around the same time requires cooked quinces to be stamped fine with almonds, curds, raisins, sugar, spices, egg yolks and butter.[12] This manuscript also contains a cheesecake known as English tart for which curd cheese, butter and egg yolks are flavoured with rose-water and baked in a case, then topped with more rose-water, sugar and butter and rebaked. A more complicated recipe, from 1612,[13] calls for *recotten* made from sheep's milk to be steeped for a few hours in goat's milk then mixed with ground pine nuts, sugar, eggs and ginger as well as puréed apples or quinces and baked in a pastry case. We are told that the result can be eaten warm or cold. Baked curd cheesecakes have long been a standard item in Dutch Jewish cooking but the mainstream has tended to ignore them, except as an occasional flan filling. Curd cheese, almost always quark, is most popularly used in unbaked cheesecakes set with gelatine; and the best ones are naturally flavoured with puréed fruit. Baked cream cheesecakes have been growing in popularity in the past few decades and are often made at home, stimulated by the local producer of American-style cream cheese and championed by women's magazines. The following flan is guiltless – the quark gives a refreshingly tangy taste and it has nowhere near the calories of a cream cheesecake.

Oven: 200°C ♦ Time: 35–45 minutes
Tin: 24 cm round sandwich tin, sides at least 4 cm high, greased

1 quantity single crust flan dough
300g quark or smooth curd cheese, full fat
3 eggs, beaten
150g sugar
1 tbsp cornflour, dissolved in very little water
zest of ½ lemon

Make the dough as described in the basic recipe. Combine the filling ingredients well and use to fill the risen dough case. Be careful not to spill any around the edges – it will brown very quickly and burn. Smooth the top and bake for 35–45 minutes until golden. Remove carefully from the tin and cool on a wire rack.

Chapter Seven

BISCUITS
Koekjes

The Dutch use two words for biscuit: *biscuit*, pronounced like the French *biscuit* from which it was taken, and that very typical word *koekje* which literally means 'little cake'. These words convey the Dutch feeling about the biscuits associated with their country. The imported French word means mass-produced dry biscuits like Marie and Nice, while the Dutch word captures the imagination with delicious promise, whether home-made or bought by weight from the baker. This is the word that Dutch settlers took to America and which subsequently became 'cookie' in American usage.[1]

Some of the earliest home-made biscuits, when they were not made in a wafer iron, were fried in a skillet or cooked on a griddle. Both of these types still exist in Holland, once popular regional specialities, now endangered species. *Drabbelkoek* is a Frisian biscuit which is now only made in culinary museums and by one or two artisanal producers. It is made from a wheat and buckwheat batter swirled through a four-holed funnel into hot fat. It is fried and pressed into a teacup to harden in a nest shape. The funnels, once part of standard Frisian kitchen equipment, have become a rarity, if not extinct. *Kruukplaetjes*, *kruu'plaetjes* and *kruudplaetjes* are all local names for the old-fashioned spiced griddle biscuits made in the South Holland/Zeeland border region. Unless enough mothers continue teaching their daughters how to make them they may soon become only a memory. Bakers don't make them any more; they require very low, prolonged heat and take up too much time to be profitable. They can be bought in the region, ordered in advance from one of the local tourist bureaux, handmade by local housewives.[2] They are made from a rich pastry-like dough and owe their typical flavour to *rommelkruid* – literally 'mess spice' – a mixture of spices including cinnamon, aniseed and white pepper. *Rommelkruid* also imparts a reddish tinge to dishes and is used in various sweet and savoury recipes including a well-known speciality called *balkenbrij*, a pâté made from a freshly slaughtered pig's head cooked with stock and buckwheat or wheat flour.

Bakers and cooks in wealthy households which possessed an oven had baked biscuits for centuries. The earliest ones were the little honey cakes like the *taai-taai* described in the *Sinterklaas* section on page 161. As sugar became more readily available, it was added in increasing proportions to biscuit doughs, resulting in the crisp structure we now almost automatically associate with biscuits. In fact, crisp may a charitable description; some doughs appear to have been downright hard, characterized by a paucity of butter. Just over 60g butter to 250g of both sugar and flour for pretzels and not quite 50g of butter to 200g sugar and 250g flour for spiced letter-biscuits seem to have been quite typical.[3] By the middle of the nineteenth century, butter had become increasingly more important as an ingredient, together with the now easily accessible sugar. In the 1850 book I mentioned earlier, *Betje the Cheap Kitchenmaid*, tea biscuits require 300g flour and 125g sugar to be mixed with 75g butter[4] and butter cookies use this amount of butter to 30g sugar and 250g flour.[5] But these are sober examples; the book gives a recipe for cream biscuits, requiring equal proportions of butter and flour (a little sugar is sprinkled on before baking), and a recipe for bishop's biscuits is so rich, with slightly more butter than flour, that it has to be baked in moulds.[6]

Good butter continues to be a major requirement for most biscuits. Some contain so much that a nugget of dough flows out to a golden circle with crisp brown edges, like the Amsterdam speciality *koggetjes*, studded with bits of caramelized sugar, and the thin and delicate *cocosgalettes* made with fine dessicated coconut. The *kletskop*, 'chatterbox', flows so much that little craters appear all over it. If you wonder why these biscuits are called chatterboxes, chew one in company and see conversation stop dead. They look like unrolled brandy snaps but they have a personality of their own and inspire strong feelings – you either love them or hate them. Significantly, people with good teeth are among their most fervent admirers. The butter and sugar cook to the consistency of hard toffee and that, combined with the nuts, gives a marvellous crunch. In Leiden, where they have always been popular, they were often referred to as *zerehoofdjes*, meaning headaches. In 1602, a similar biscuit called a *kanteling* inspired poet Zaccharias Heyns to compose the following remarkable lines:

Kantelingen,
Dat zijn van die hooge spitse dinghen,
Die ons Schorftenhoofdjes noemt,
Doch sijn se met suyker en caneel bebloemt,
Noyt beter cost en hebt ghy gheten.[7]

Kantelings,
They are tall pointy things,
Scabby Heads, so they are known,
But strewn with sugar and cinnamon I own,
You've never eaten any thing so good.

This graphic description leaves little doubt that it is a form of *kletskop*, but it was probably rolled up like a brandy snap. *Kant*, incidentally, means lace, the biscuit name apparently inspired by the pattern of the finished product.

A mixture of butter biscuits, often sold loose by weight, is referred to as *roomboter allerhande*, 'butter allsorts', and can contain various flavours and shapes often embellished with nuts and chocolate. *Javaantjes* ('little Javans') are flavoured with coffee and cut into a pointed oval shape. Many places in Holland distinguish themselves with a local version of the *sprits*, a piped butter biscuit. Most are quite similar to each other, often just piped in a different shape, but two are distinctive. The *Utrechtse sprits* is generously laced with salt, and this salt/sweet combination somehow makes it very moreish. The accepted shape is a zigzag which is portioned after baking, but a few bakers pipe it in serrated batons. It has been a speciality of Utrecht since the 1890s when it was supposedly introduced by a local baker, Pieter Bergman, who had worked in Germany where this type of biscuit was very popular.[8] *Blauwvingers,* 'blue fingers', are peculiar to Zwolle. They are piped in wide serrated batons and are indented at one end while they are still soft. This hollow is filled with melted chocolate and the biscuit does rather resemble a finger – one with a hideously dirty fingernail! The name *blauwvinger* comes from a popular nickname for the inhabitants of Zwolle and there is a colourful legend as to how they got it. In the Middle Ages a bitter feud raged between the cities of Zwolle and Kampen, and the inhabitants never lost an opportunity to get the better of each other. When the church tower in Zwolle was destroyed by a fire, the bells remained intact and were sold. Kampen bought them, purposely paying the full sum in small denomination copper coins. By the time they had finished counting the money, the citizens of Zwolle had blue fingers, both from the cold and from the metal rubbing off onto them.[9] The name *sprits* or *spris* has existed for centuries in Holland, but the original delicacy was a choux-like confection which was baked in a tin or forced into hot butter[10] and eaten with powdered sugar. This kind of fritter is now known as a snowball and the batter is often studded with dried fruit. As its name implies, it is liberally dusted with icing sugar before being served. Other kinds of biscuits also went under the name *sprits,* and Gerrit van den Brenk gives several versions. In addition to the forced choux confection mentioned above there are *Marzepain-sprits*, predictably made from a marzipan-like mixture which is forced through a pump onto sugar-strewn paper. *Orangje-sprits* on the other hand, is more like a present-day *Weespermop*, with the added flavouring of finely chopped candied orange peel and citron. It is sliced from a roll and is, in the eyes of its originator, *'heel mooy voor het oog'*: very pleasing to the eye.

Almond biscuits are eaten in prodigious quantities and the chewy bitter almond macaroon, *bitterkoekje*, has always been a prime favourite in Holland. In the early nineteenth century, a bedtime glass of milk might even contain crushed macaroons instead of the more usual aniseed, sage or chocolate.[11] For centuries they were served at weddings, their bitter-sweetness symbolizing life. Nowadays they are eaten on their own and are also used in many puddings and cake fillings; they are even added to cake batter. The baker buys his paste ready-made from a wholesaler and only needs to add egg white. This paste has a percentage of bitter almonds and is not readily available to the public. However, the macaroons are very simple to make using ground almonds and bitter almond extract. Bitter almonds are difficult to get hold of because of the, admittedly slight, risk of poisoning. Bakers of old were seemingly much readier to sacrifice public health on the altar of taste; Gerrit van den Brink specifies equal amounts of sweet and bitter almonds for his *bittere koekjes*.To reassure you, macaroons are made from a heated mixture, therefore the prussic acid contained in the raw kernel of bitter almonds evaporates. Vanilla nuts use a similar mixture to macaroons but require more patience as the piped paste must dry for several hours before an incision is made into the top of each one. The soft insides then flow out in a rather macabre fashion when they are baked. Many other types of almond biscuits are made from a raw mixture with the consistency of almond paste, piped into distinctive patterns and garnished with nuts and chocolate or even jam.

Crisp meringues are found in various forms, flavoured with fruit extracts, coffee, nuts and cocoa. Recipes haven't changed significantly. A 1746 cookery book as well as one from 1850 give similar recipes for meringue-like *nonneveesjes*, one flavoured with orange blossom,[12] the other with lemon zest.[13] The later book also gives a rather remarkable recipe for *schuimptjes* – remarkable because the word is used in contemporary Dutch for meringue – in which egg yolks are whisked with cream and sugar, flavoured with coffee or cocoa and baked in moulds.

Biscuits are still the everyday accompaniment to a mid-morning cup of coffee or a cup of tea in the afternoon. This combination, now commonplace, can be traced back to the latter part of the seventeenth century when the two beverages, first tea then coffee, began to reach all levels of society. From the outset, they were not drunk at an accepted mealtime.[14] Instead, a new meal was created, one that radiated luxury, especially attracting better-situated city-dwellers. Both drinks were expensive and were taken with the almost equally costly sugar. Country people might have an afternoon snack of coffee or tea with rusks or bread and cheese; their city cousins ate cakes, pastries and biscuits.[15] It became something of a status symbol to give tea parties, reflecting one's social standing as well as one's bank balance. Exquisite porcelain tea-sets, Japanese or Venetian dishes, golden spoons and forks were deemed necessary to serve the tea and its accompanying delicacies.[16] It was a social event and hostesses vied with each other to produce delectable morsels. *Confituren* were served in various forms: fruit might be candied, or pulp might be cooked with sugar and spread to dry in a thin sheet;[17] or the resulting jam-like confection might be poured into teacups or special little moulds to set.[18] As time went on, biscuits of the kind we recognize today began to increase in popularity, the ideal partner for the endless cups of tea and social visits that were the rage in fashionable circles.

CINNAMON BISCUITS WITH ALMONDS
Janhagel

Janhagel is a very popular biscuit, even abroad. The two components of the name mean literally 'John' and 'hail'. *Janhagel* is an obsolete seventeenth-century expression which means 'the man in the street'.[19] This recipe is for the most popular type, the kind anyone would recognize under that name. The sugar nibs in the topping, called 'hail sugar' in Dutch, were very likely contrived as a topping because of the name. This, however, is a newer invention. The old *Janhagel*, difficult to find nowadays, is a cross between a spice cake and a biscuit, made from rye flour and honey with an attractively cobbled surface. They are time-consuming to make by hand in large batches as even-sized pellets must be cut in huge quantities. These pellets spread into each other on baking, producing the desired cobbled effect. Some bakers used specially designed 'cannons' (also used to cut the *Sinterklaas* speciality *pepernoten*) which look like large meat mincers. The pellets fly out at one end, shaped and ready to be put on sheets. An older and simpler aid was a wooden plank with a cobbled pattern cut into it, so the biscuits could be shaped and baked like hand-made *speculaas*.

Oven: 180°C ♦ Tin: 1 sheet, 25 x 35 cm ♦ Time: about 20 minutes
Yield: 2 dozen biscuits

150g butter, softened	*$1/2$ tsp baking powder*
100g caster sugar	*$1/4$ tsp salt*
1 beaten egg	*1 tsp cinnamon*
225g all-purpose flour	*50g sugar nibs or white sugar candy*
	75g sliced almonds

Cream the butter and sugar together until lightened in colour. Sift the flour, baking powder, salt and cinnamon together and add to the creamed mixture with half the egg. Knead lightly until it comes together. Cut a sheet of baking parchment to fit the tin. Turn the dough out onto the paper and roll it out evenly to fit. This is the easiest way, as the dough is thin and will almost certainly break if you move it without support. Place the paper with the dough on the baking sheet. Brush with the rest of the beaten egg and sprinkle the sugar over the dough. Scatter the almonds evenly over the dough. Press lightly with your hands to embed the topping as well as possible. Bake for about 20 minutes. Place the paper with the biscuit sheet on a cutting surface and cut into 24 rectangles measuring 3 x 8 cm. Remove from the paper and cool on wire racks. Store in an airtight container.

FRISIAN THUMBS
Friese Dumkes

These chunky fingers do resemble thumbs, especially if an indentation is made at one end as some people like. The biscuits are spicy and nutty and very moreish and – best of all – they are whipped up in minutes. For an extra special treat, drizzle with or dip in melted bittersweet chocolate – not traditional, but absolutely delicious!

Oven: 180°C ◆ Tin: 1 sheet, greased ◆ Time: about 15 minutes
Yield: 2 dozen biscuits

125g all-purpose flour
$^1/_8$ tsp salt
50g hazelnuts, finely chopped
$^1/_2$ tsp ground cinnamon
$^1/_2$ tsp ginger

$^1/_2$ tsp ground aniseed
1 tsp whole aniseed (optional)
50g soft dark brown sugar
60g butter, softened
2 tbsp beaten egg + 1 tbsp water

Sift the dry ingredients together. Add the butter, egg and water and knead lightly until it all comes together. Roll out to a thickness of 1 cm and cut into 2 x 5 cm fingers. Arrange on the baking sheet and bake for about 15 minutes. Remove from the sheet and cool on a wire rack. Store in an airtight container. They are best eaten fresh.

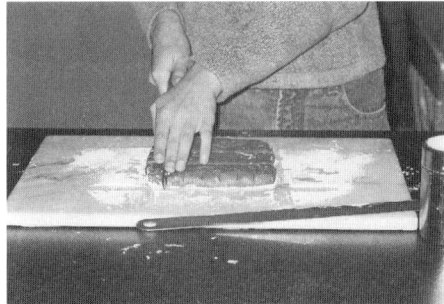

ALMOND-PASTE SANDWICH
Gevulde koeken

These delicious biscuits have got be the nation's Number One Bestseller and, tragically, this popularity is dangerously close to destroying them. Everybody makes them: the local baker at the corner, the market baker and the biscuit manufacturer, hence the quality of the ingredients varies greatly, with cheap pulses or apricot kernels replacing the almonds in the filling and margarine the butter in the pastry. Even more people sell them; you can buy them loose or prepackaged, even individually packaged, from the baker, the supermarket, the railway station restaurant and the school canteen. Often, the name is the only common characteristic. This recipe is for the genuine article, pure and simple.

Oven: 200°C ♦ Tin: sheet, greased and floured ♦ Time: about 20 minutes
Yield: 1 dozen biscuits

Pastry:
250g all-purpose flour
1 tsp baking powder
$^1/_4$ tsp salt
160g butter, cubed
125g caster sugar
zest of $^1/_2$ lemon
$^1/_2$ beaten egg

Filling:
275g almond paste
approx. $^1/_2$ beaten egg

Additional:
egg for glazing
12 blanched almonds

Put the flour, baking powder and salt in a large bowl. Rub in the butter until the mixture resembles fine breadcrumbs. Mix in the sugar and lemon zest. Add the egg and knead very lightly until it comes together. Set aside for about 15 minutes in a cool place.

Mix the almond paste with enough beaten egg to make it malleable. Divide into twelve portions. Roll each portion into a ball and flatten slightly between your hands to a diameter of 5 cm. Set aside.

On a floured surface roll the pastry out to about 30 x 45 cm. The pastry is quite short and may crack, but it will reseal if you press the cracks gently together. Use a fluted 7 cm cutter to cut out circles as economically as possible. Reroll any trimmings and recut. You need 24 circles of pastry. Space 12 of the circles evenly on the baking sheet. Top with a disc of almond paste. Moisten the edges of the pastry with water and cover with the other 12 pieces. Press gently with your fingertips to seal. The amount of filling is generous but it is worth spending the little extra time coaxing the pastry around it. Brush with beaten egg and top with an almond. Leave to rest for about 15 minutes before baking. Bake for about 20 minutes until golden brown. Cool on a wire rack. Store in an airtight container.

SQUARE SAND BISCUITS
Pitmoppen

The word *mop* is used for dozens of biscuits. The *Weespermop* is made from almond paste and egg alone, rolled into a cylinder and cut into rounds. *Gooise moppen* are buttery and are sliced from a chilled slab into rectangles. *Goudse moppen* are flavoured with lemon and are sliced from a roll. The following *Pitmoppen* are mellow-tasting with a flavour that always reminds me of custard creams.

Oven: 180°C ♦ Tin: 2 sheets, well greased ♦ Time: 15–20 minutes
Yield: 42 biscuits

175g butter, softened	*250g all-purpose flour*
125g caster sugar	*$^{1}/_{2}$ tsp baking powder*
$^{1}/_{2}$ beaten egg	*$^{1}/_{4}$ tsp salt*
1 tsp vanilla extract	*84 blanched almonds*

Cream the butter and sugar together until pale. Add the other ingredients (not the almonds) and knead lightly until they come together. Place on a floured plate and chill for about 15 minutes. Roll the dough to a 24 x 28 cm rectangle on a floured worktop. Use a sharp knife or pastry wheel with a plain blade to cut 42 4 x 4 cm squares and arrange these on the baking sheets. Press two almonds into each square. Bake until golden brown. Remove and cool on wire racks. Store in an airtight container.

Making pretzels. Behind the sign pictured on the opposite page lurks this giant pretzel-rolling machine. Two lines of dough are rolled progressively thinner as they pass under three rollers on the slope. They are cut into pretzel-sized pieces by the guillotines at the bottom. Each piece is rolled again to make a long string. These can be seen piling up (liberally sugared to stop them sticking to each other) at the back of the work bench. Here, Berry the baker gives them a finishing touch before tying the characteristic knot (see the next page). The rolling machine was designed and built by Berry's grandfather, the founder of this bakery some 80 years ago. Towering behind the rolling machine can be seen the mechanical proofer. This enables Berry to work single-handed.

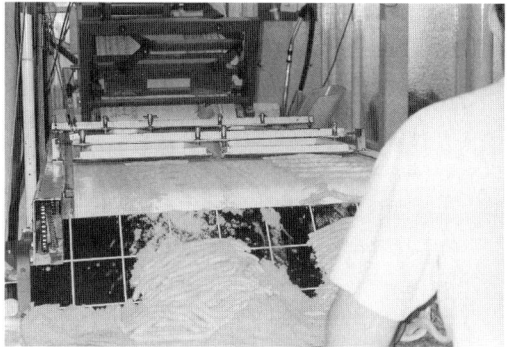

SWEET PRETZELS
Krakelingen

The pretzel, which supposedly spread to the rest of Europe from Italy,[20] has been a baker's symbol since time immemorial and Holland is no exception. However, while most other countries have savoury pretzels, Dutch ones are almost always sweet. The choux pretzels, made up to the previous century for funerals in some parts of Friesland,[21] are now only a memory. Nowadays most people prefer the buttery, soft-textured, hand-rolled yeast pretzels or the mechanically-cut, pastry biscuit ones but, until this century, pretzels were usually hard or crisp. The name *krakeling* is linguistically related both to the verb *kraken*, to crack or crunch, and the noun *krakeel*, meaning quarrel or fight. Old Dutch paintings are full of pretzels and, when they are not a passive part of a still life, they are often portrayed as the centrepiece of a game in which two people each hook their little finger into an end and pull to see who will come away with most. This figures, among others, in Pieter Bruegel's painting featuring Dutch proverbs and the intended expression, *'se trecken om't lanxte eind'* in Old Dutch, translates literally as 'they are pulling for the longer end'. The current expression uses the opposite adjective and *'aan het kortste eind trekken'* means to get the short end of the stick. They were also popular in portraits of children, the image of a pretzel symbolizing hands folded in prayer underlining the innocence being portrayed.

An eighteenth-century recipe describes a dough made from flour, egg yolks and a moderate amount of butter, flavoured with coriander and rose-water, shaped into pretzels, baked and dried in the oven[22] to produce a hard biscuit. Tastes have changed. The village church, perennially in need of

Making pretzels, part II. Berry ties the knots and lays them out on a baking tray. He sprinkles the tray with more sugar (some has already been rolled automatically into the dough as it passed through the final rolling process) and presses it into the biscuits with a hand-held board. In the bottom photograph, a tray has been baked satisfactorily and will be transferred to the cooling rack pictured on page 122. Helped by all his machines, Berry can turn out up to 4000 pretzels a day, six days a week. His work may include special orders, such as the giant numerals being prepared for a 50th birthday, illustrated on page 121.

money, holds several door-to-door sales every year. On each of these occasions, a single product is offered, often bakery items like biscuits and wafers, or the delicious pretzels made by a baker in a nearby town who uses a unique recipe inherited from his grandfather. Although the kneading and portioning are done by customized machinery, it remains a time-consuming process as each pretzel is then hand-rolled. The church ladies bag them, eight to a little greaseproof bag, before sallying forth to pamper the village's sweet tooth. The baskets are emptied in a flash: no one can resist their buttery caramel flavour. The recipe below, my own concoction, can be varied at will to make a softer or crisper biscuit by playing with the baking time. Some bakers use a recipe and method similar to the one for brown sugar coils on page 53, making the pretzels far smaller than the coils. The result is a softer, more bread-like biscuit. If the dough is rolled into an exceedingly long rope you get a *magere man*, 'thin man', an exaggeratedly elongated pretzel.

Oven: 220°C ♦ Time: 10–15 minutes ♦ Yield: 32 small pretzels
Tin: 2 baking sheets, lined with non-stick baking parchment

250g strong white flour	*50 ml milk, warmed to 37°C*
1 ¼ tsp easyblend yeast	*100g butter, melted then cooled*
2 tbsp sugar	*1 egg, lightly beaten*
¼ tsp salt	*175–200g soft light brown sugar*

Mix the flour, yeast, 2 tbsp sugar and salt in a large bowl. Add the milk, melted butter and beaten egg and mix with a spoon or spatula until the dry ingredients are well moistened. Knead it well, in the bowl or on a suitable surface, but don't add any flour. The dough is soft and very malleable and responds well to kneading. Shape into a ball and put it in the bowl. Cover with a teatowel wrung out in hot water and leave in a warm draught-free place until doubled in bulk. Be patient – it is rich and will take a little longer than bread dough.

Scatter the light brown sugar onto an extra baking sheet or tray. Knock back the dough, knead it lightly and divide into 32 pieces. Toss the pieces in the sugar and roll each piece out to a rope anywhere between 25 to 30 cm. They will shrink a little as soon as you stop rolling, so bear that in mind. The longer the rope, the slimmer and more shapely the pretzel. Roll each rope around in the sugar and leave to rest there while you make the others. Try to roll the dough pieces and ropes around in the sugar as much as possible, so that the sugar 'sweats' into the dough. When you've rolled 16 ropes, start shaping them into pretzels and place them on the lined baking sheet. Then continue with the rest of the dough. Leave the shaped pretzels to rest, covered and out of the draught, for about half an hour before baking them. The longer you bake them the crisper they get, so if you like a softer biscuit, reduce the baking time. Leave to cool on the sheets. Store in an airtight container.

Chapter Eight

PANCAKES
Pannenkoeken

ancakes are popular in Holland, both at home and out and about.
Pancake houses offer dozens – even hundreds – of kinds whose
main difference is generally in the topping combination, generally
of fruit, cheese or preserved meats. These modest resorts are often found
on the fringe of woods or parks and there always seems to be something
nostalgic in the atmosphere, something comfortingly old-fashioned. The
pancakes they serve range from exotic to homely. Even what we call
homely are a far cry from those eaten in the past, when pancakes were to
be found at two opposing ends of the scale: a hearty and nourishing
workingman's food or a featherlight omelette-like *struif* which graced the
tables of the rich as a dessert dish. *Struiven* were made from eggs, sugar
and milk or cream, bound with a variety of ingredients ranging from a
spoonful or two of fine flour to rusk crumbs or white breadcrumbs. Egg
whites were usually whisked separately to lend lightness. Ground almonds
might be added, or puréed fruits like redcurrants, apples and rosehips.[1] By
the end of the nineteenth century, recipes for *struiven* had become more like
pancakes, with more generous amounts of flour, but the whites were still
whisked separately.[2] And there is one recipe for egg pancakes which is a
hybrid, with the yolks whisked for 10 minutes with sugar, the whites folded
in at the end.[3]

The dish *panckoecken* was known in the Middle Ages, but it was more
like a fritter or a New Year's Eve *oliebol*. Recipes called for fine flour and
yeast to be made into a dough and rolled out as thinly as possible, sometimes studded with a few currants or pieces of apple. They were most likely
deep-fried.[4] Rice pancakes were also made to various recipes. Rice might

be boiled in milk and left to stand overnight, presumably to ferment a little, before mixing in eggs and as much wheat flour as was required;[5] or very thick rice porridge could be mixed with eggs, cinnamon and rusk crumbs and fried as smaller cakes.[6] Shrove Tuesday celebrations for most people invariably included pancakes, as in so many other countries, and there was a widespread tradition of going from house to house to sing for a pancake, often directly, like in this early seventeenth-century Amsterdam verse:

> Gheef mij een pankoeck uit de pan,
> Ho, man, ho!
> De Vastelavont die komt an…[7]

> *Give me a pancake from the pan,*
> *Ho, man, ho!*
> *Shrove Tuesday's coming…*

For several centuries simple pancakes were widely eaten as a meal in themselves, especially in rural communities in the east of the country. Here, the sandy soil was poor but supported the undemanding buckwheat which was used to make pancakes. In the province of Drenthe, rye was sometimes added to the batter.[8] But the Second World War brought about significant changes in Dutch eating habits. Modern agricultural techniques meant that poor soil could be artificially enhanced and more profitable crops soon replaced much of the buckwheat. Self-sufficiency was no longer as widespread and the pancake-meal declined. It needn't have. Perhaps the association of pancakes with poverty and deprivation was still too acute, because that is what pancakes had traditionally been for many: a stopgap or convenience meal, always a cheap, yet nourishing, alternative. Whole hamlets and villages were often infused with the smell of pancakes, not that delicious buttery smell that conjures them for us, but the pungent odour of poverty, of home-grown buckwheat mixed with skimmed milk and fried in the cheapest rapeseed oil. More fortunate souls might afford creamy milk

and fresh eggs to enrich the batter, but these were more often sold for ready money not kept for home consumption in poor labourers' families. Even a bit of bacon or a little dripping were beyond the reach of some.

Though the preparation itself required good planning and could be time-consuming, pancakes offered several advantages. To be eaten in the morning, the batter would be made the night before; then the leavening – though they were not invariably leavened – could work at its leisure.[9] Pancakes once made, could be reheated later or even eaten cold. They were most popular as a breakfast dish.[10] As it was customary for early-rising countryfolk to have two or three breakfasts, pancakes saved on the far more expensive bread, and made a welcome change from yet another plate of potatoes or porridge. They were cheap, usually made from home-produced ingredients, and didn't necessarily require a filling or topping. In addition, they were extremely sustaining and could be taken into the fields, a great convenience at busy times. They also provided welcome nourishment during the months when labour was not required and consequently no ready money was available, even for such basics as food. Then they would take the place of bread and might even replace the main meal as the stock of root vegetables began to dwindle.

When pancakes were eaten as a dessert, they usually followed a meal of pulses, either whole or in soup form. This is puzzling inasmuch as Dutch pea soup is a thick and filling affair, often eaten with equally substantial coarse rye bread. This tradition has not completely died out and I have been told by more than one person that when they were growing up it was customary to follow split-pea soup with pancakes, statements borne out by sociological studies.[11] I found confirmation when I opened a late nine-teenth-century cookery book and a yellowed newspaper-cutting fell out. It was undated and, though by no means as old as the book, the antiquated spelling placed it around the early to middle twentieth century. It was a recipe for thick pea soup with accompanying instructions for pancakes. Somewhat confusingly, the recipe writer uses the diminutive form for pan-cakes, even though describing one large pancake fried at a time. Though without a name, the list of ingredients leaves little doubt that he or she was suggesting three-in-the-pan pancakes, described below on page 129.

There was great regional variety in the past: some types have become extinct, others are now only made as a curiosity. *Gieterse* or *Giethoornse pannenkoeken* are among those still enjoyed on a fairly frequent basis today. These rather heavy, thin, unleavened buckwheat pancakes are a speciality of Giethoorn, a picturesque town in Drenthe, often referred to as the Venice of Holland because of its abundance of waterways. Another speciality of Drenthe, *maaierspannenkoek*, 'reaper's pancake', was also made with buckwheat, with a rusk or two crumbled into the rich batter.

Some were made for a special occasion in a particular place, like the *refoelen* from IJsselmonde which were eaten at calving time.[12] Thin pancakes were spread with a mixture of colostrum, brown sugar, steeped raisins and currants, and crumbs of fine rye bread and cinnamon, or crumbled spice cake. They were eaten either hot or completely cold. The *vetkoeken*, 'fat cakes', of Zeeland have gone out of fashion too. Recipes call for a rich yeasted batter, with raisins and currants, to be fried as small cakes, like a thicker version of three-in-the-pan pancakes. To finish, they are dredged liberally with white or brown sugar and cut into strips, then eaten.[13] *Groeninger pannenkoecken*, wheat cakes enriched with currants and cinnamon and fried in butter, were a treat which appeared in print as early as 1668,[14] and *Gooische pannenkoeken*, made from a thin but rich batter, appear to have been a favourite in the eighteenth and nineteenth centuries.[15] *Rietperen pannenkoeken*, pear pancakes, once widespread all over the country, and especially popular in the provinces of North and South Holland,[16] are but a memory. The pears were stewed and then covered with a yeasted batter.

Pancakes have now become a treat. Far from viewing it as a hardship, children eagerly look forward to the occasions when they may replace a main meal. The modern housewife no longer has to squat in front of a blazing fire with her long-handled frying pan like the toothless crones in old paintings, nor does she have to labour over a sooty wood-burning stove. Pancakes have come full circle and are now a convenience food of a modern age. Supermarket shelves are stocked with pancake mixes to suit all tastes and few people bother to make them from scratch. Buckwheat and grains like oats and barley have remained important ingredients and pancakes are still eaten in the traditional way, with *stroop*. Though you can still buy pure beet molasses (*stroop*) from healthfood shops, usually some refined sugars are now added. The real thing is extremely rich in iron. In the past, it supplied nutritional value to otherwise meagre diets. It was a household remedy, too, curing all sorts of things from coughs to constipation.[17] Long before sugar from beet, cane sugar was processed in the numerous refineries in Holland. Still before that, the juice of fruit like apples and pears was boiled down to an almost black mass with a consistency somewhere between molasses and jam. *Appel-* and *perenstroop* are still made and eaten, but no longer on such a large scale. Modern children are developing a taste for refined syrups and icing sugar.[18] The tang of bitter-sweet molasses complements the flavour of the pancakes, even savoury ones made with bacon. It confuses the tastebuds less than the New World custom of eating pancakes with refined syrup and bacon on the side. *Stroopsaus*, molasses sauce, has gone out of fashion – our bodies no longer welcome the extra calories. This warm sauce, made by mixing molasses

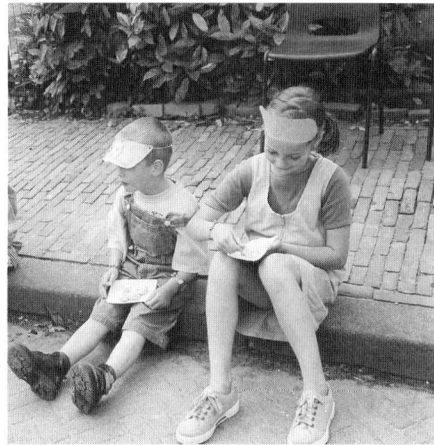

A domestic poffertje-*pan (top left) is dwarfed by the giant set-up (housed in a trailer) that was cooking* poffertjes *for all-comers at the Zuidlaren horse fair (top right). The street has been closed for a 'play-day' and the* poffertje-*maker has arrived. He cooks them on a medium-sized griddle and the children are happy to squat on the kerb to wolf them down.*

with dripping was a popular accompaniment in the past. Feel free to top the pancakes in this chapter with anything you like, but do try the beet molasses if at all possible. It is rather an acquired taste, but you might like it – at the worst you'll be an experience richer!

Not all pancakes are eaten with *stroop* or even syrup. *Poffertjes*, tiny puff pancakes, need just melted butter and icing sugar. They are a popular feature at open-air festivities and markets, made while you wait, on huge griddles which look like an endless expanse of shallow egg boxes. Deft fingers squirt batter into the indentations, flipping the pancakes over as soon as they set. They are made regularly in most households too, in special frying pans: using a plastic puff-pancake batter-squeezer minimizes mess and ensures an accurate dose of the batter.

BACON PANCAKES
Spekpannenkoeken

This kind of pancake, often plain, formed the basis of many a country-dweller's diet before the Second World War, especially those who worked the fields; it was nourishing food that stuck to the ribs. Putting in the bacon made it more of a treat:[19] few Frisian harvest meals were complete without them.[20] The modern stomach will find one or two of the pancakes made to this recipe more than enough, but accounts speak of a diameter of 50 cm and a thickness of 2–4 cm as no rarity. A labourer would eat about a quarter of one and even then might have a slice or two of coarse rye bread to fill up the empty spaces.[21] This particular pancake, unsubtle in itself, could also form part of a delicate and discreet courtship ritual, and could answer a proposal of marriage without a word being exchanged. In the Betuwe for example, a girl consented by covering the bacon completely with batter – visible bits of bacon were a bad sign.[22] This custom was not confined to bacon pancakes. In Friesland a pancake topped with butter and sugar conveyed a warmth of feeling totally lacking in the alternative of dripping and molasses. This batter can also be used for apple pancakes.

Yield: about 6 pancakes 25 cm across

125g all-purpose flour	1/4 tsp salt
125g buckwheat flour	1 egg, beaten
3/4 tsp easyblend yeast	450 ml lukewarm milk
1/2 tsp sugar	125g very thinly sliced streaky bacon
	butter for frying

Mix the dry ingredients together in a large bowl and whisk in the eggs and about a third of the milk, adding the rest gradually. Cover the lump-free mixture with a damp tea towel and leave in a warm place for about an hour. It should look frothy. Whisk again before using. For each pancake, melt some butter in a well-seasoned skillet or non-stick pan. Add about 100 ml batter and swirl to coat the pan. Arrange some bacon on top and flip over as soon as the top has set. Invert onto a plate as soon as the bacon has had a chance to cook. For apple pancakes, slice the apples very thinly, or they will fall out as the pancakes are flipped over. Follow the same procedure as for bacon pancakes.

THREE-IN-THE-PAN FRUIT PANCAKES
Drie-in-de-pan

Three of these pancakes fit into an average sized frying pan – hence the name. This recipe is an old-fashioned one with buckwheat. The trend today is to use only white flour and sometimes the yeast is replaced with baking powder. This is seen as a shortcut, but the only thing longer about the traditional recipe is the resting time. Use a nonstick frying pan or a well-seasoned iron skillet.

Yield: 12–15 pancakes

150g all-purpose flour   *300 ml milk, warmed to 37°C*
150g buckwheat flour   *1 egg, well beaten*
1 ¹/₂ tsp easyblend yeast   *25g–50g each, currants and sultanas*
¹/₄ tsp salt   *¹/₂ apple, finely chopped*
2 tsp sugar   *butter for frying*
     caster or icing sugar for dusting

Wash and dry the currants and sultanas. Put the flours, yeast, salt and sugar in a large bowl. Add the beaten egg and the milk a little at a time and whisk to a smooth batter. Add the currants, sultanas and apple and mix well. Cover the bowl with a damp tea towel and leave to rest for an hour. Heat some butter in the frying pan and use a serving-spoon to apportion the batter. Make 3 pancakes per batch. Turn them over as soon as they start to set and small bubbles appear. Remember that too much heat will burn them without cooking the insides; too little will make them rubbery. Eat warm, with a generous dusting of icing or caster sugar.

Most Dutch fêtes, bazaars, bring-and-buys and so forth have something on offer to eat: not just cakes and a cup of tea, but pancakes, waffles, wafers and all that sort of thing will be cooked to order. Here is the pancake-stall at my local church sale of work, where they were being offered with icing sugar or with stroop, the beet molasses so popular with the Dutch.

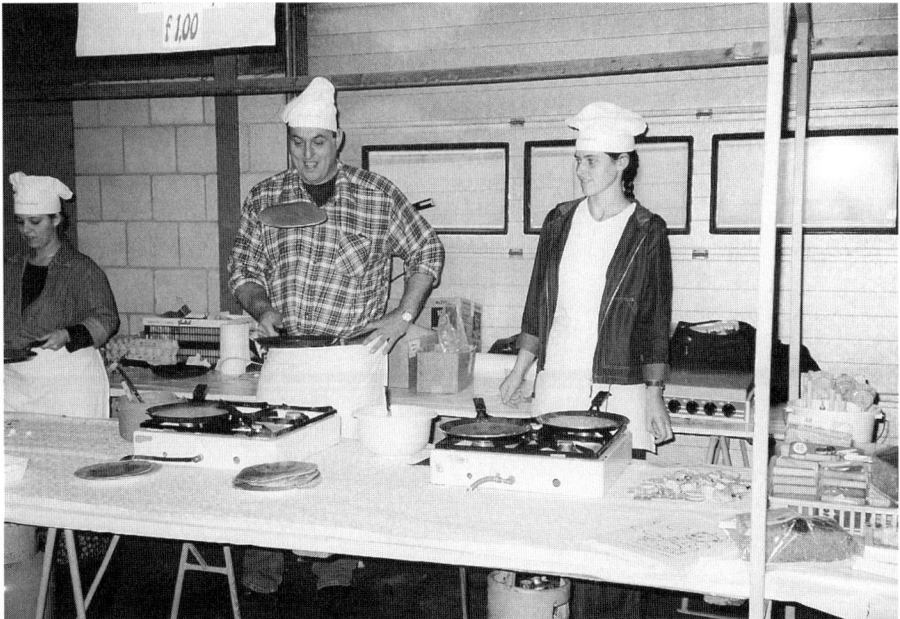

CHERRY PANCAKES
Kersenpannenkoeken

These pancakes are a popular southern Dutch treat.

Yield: 7 or 8 pancakes 25 cm across

250g all-purpose flour	*3 eggs*
$1/_2$ tsp baking powder	*400 ml milk*
pinch of salt	*500g pitted cherries, halved*

Mix the flour, baking powder and salt together in a large bowl and whisk in the eggs with about half of the milk, adding the rest gradually. Melt some butter in a nonstick frying pan. Add a ladleful of batter and swirl to coat the pan. Scatter cherry halves on this and press gently to embed them in the batter. Turn the pancake as soon as it has set. If the cherries have been well pressed in you can do it with a wide palette knife or fish-slice but if you're nervous, turn it upside down onto a well-oiled dinner plate and slide it back into the frying pan. Don't leave it in the pan for too long or the cherries will blacken. Re-invert to serve, dredged with caster or icing sugar.

Stroopwafels.

Chapter Nine

WAFFLES AND WAFERS
Wafels

The Dutch word *wafel*, from which the English word waffle is derived, covers both the thick raised waffles of the English-speaking world as well as thin and delicate wafers, with a range of textures between these two extremes. Wafers and waffles have been made in Holland for several centuries. The oldest existing wafer iron on display in Holland is the sixteenth-century one taken by Anna van Buren to the household of her husband Prince Willem I,[1] but even before that, a description of wafer-making in the kitchen of the Duchess of Guelders in the fifteenth century had been committed to paper.[2] Several seventeenth-century Dutch paintings depicting convivial-looking celebrations, often Twelfth Night, give prominent place to waffles. Much as groups went carolling in Britain, Star singers, dressed as the three Wise Men, with a retinue would follow their paper star to houses where they might beg a share of the evening's waffles and pancakes.[3] Twelfth Night was one of the most popular celebrations by the late fifteenth century[4] and reached its peak in the Golden Age[5] before fading away almost altogether by the latter part of the twentieth century. But paintings give little clue as to the delicious diversity of flavour and texture: crisp, soft or even deliberately limp, spiced, oozing with butter and cream. Wafers can be crisply thin and delicate or have a definite bite, and the queen of them all, the toffee-filled wafer, defies categorization. Most waffles and wafers are a home-made tradition, but travelling Dutch waffle-makers were made welcome at feasts and festivities all over Europe in previous centuries. A set of waffle or wafer irons, and a pot for the batter, was all the equipment they needed to produce a range of mouthwatering delicacies. Even so, it must have cost some effort to travel around with them as the irons were extremely heavy. The deep waffle irons were almost invariably rectangular with square indentations; wafer irons, by contrast, were often intricately decorated.

Irons were not the exclusive preserve of the affluent. Even those in average circumstances could afford to make their own waffles and wafers, and the poor could always rely on the charity of those better situated than themselves. It was quite usual for a household to make 1000 to 1500 wafers at New Year, most of which would be given away. Not only were there the servants, labourers and their families, as well as the local clergyman and other notables, the poor too got their share. It was customary for children and poor people to go from house to house at the New Year or Twelfth Night, chanting nonsensical begging songs in various dialects, to be rewarded with wafers or waffles, depending on what part of the country they lived in. In eastern Holland they sang:

> Geluksalig Nijjaar!   *Happy New Year!*
> 'n Keukske veur mi'j klaar,   *A [wafer] biscuit ready for me here,*
> 'n Slokske der bie,   *And to go with it a tot,*
> Das goed veur mie.[6]   *That really hits the spot.*

In some villages in Brabant, the song would specifically request a waffle, which was more popular there.

Nieuwjaarke zoete,
't varkje heeft vier voeten,
Vier voeten en een staart,
Ik ben toch wel een wafel waard?[7]

New Year so sweet,
The pig has four feet,
Four feet and a tail too,
I'm surely worth a waffle from you?

If their efforts were unrewarded, they were not averse to tacking on an insulting couplet. Much earlier, the begging had grown to such proportions that church and local councils tried unsuccessfully to have it banned, as in Coevorden in 1770. By all accounts, the ensuing riot must have been a sight to behold, with angry demonstrators brandishing wafer irons threateningly, refusing to be silenced.[8] The councilmen, although their numbers were strengthened by several prominent citizens, recognized defeat, revoked the by-law on the spot and beat a retreat – hampered by their pursuers who cared not which part of anatomy or clothing they clamped between the blades of their irons.[9] The incident was to remain in public memory for some time. Etchings were made of the scene,[10] and it provided material for a farce *Burger- en Overheidsstrijd* (Civilian and Government Battle).[11] Today, children in some rural communities will still go from door to door for their wafers, not for reasons of poverty, but for the sake of folklore.

In past centuries local blacksmiths were usually charged with the task of fashioning a custom-made wafer iron, popularly given as a bridal gift by the family. All kinds of patterns were engraved, often a queer mixture of pagan and Christian symbols. Religious motifs were a constant reminder of the ecclesiastic origins claimed for the wafer as consecrated communion bread. Depictions associated with Easter were particularly common, tangible evidence of the muddle which long surrounded New Year. Although 1 January had officially marked the beginning of the year since the first century AD, clerics later started agitating for it to start on 25 December. In much of medieval Europe however, the calendar (although not necessarily the popular) year ended and began in March, or at Eastertide, and the lands of the Duke of Brabant and the Counts of Flanders and Holland fell in with this convention. An official end to some of this confusion was reached by a royal decree of 16 June 1575 which fixed New Year at 1 January.[12] Which New Year, you might ask, would be celebrated by the decorations on the wafer irons themselves: the old or the new? An iron from 1648 is engraved with a cross, initials and the date as well as a pelican feeding two young ones with its blood. Another from 1791 shows a farm waggon.[13] One from 1735 shows among other objects, a heart cut into a cross, surrounded by instruments of torture associated with the Passion, capped with the text INRI. The cross is flanked by dice and fifteen rounds, presumably representing the silver pieces. A cock roosts on a ladder, and trees of life and the slightly mangled inscription *Si Deus pro nobis Quis contra nos* are also prominent.[14] Pious texts like this were popular, varying from the concise *Geen beter lot, dan vrede met God* (No better lot than peace with God)[15] to the more admonitory:

<table>
<tr><td>Die het jaar begint,</td><td>*Whoever starts the year,*</td></tr>
<tr><td>Met lust en is gezint,</td><td>*With joy and does not fear*</td></tr>
<tr><td>Om zich tot God te wenden,</td><td>*To turn to God each day,*</td></tr>
<tr><td>Dan zal het in vreede enden.[16]</td><td>*Will end it in a peaceful way.*</td></tr>
</table>

Even a worldly warning against gluttony of various kinds could be couched in inoffensive terms, like this inscription from 1791:

Ik ben zoet en zeer begeert,

Doch ras gegeten en verteert,

Zo is 't met al het aards genot,

Bedenk dit mensch en soek na God[17]

I am sweet and arouse desire in many,

Consumed with passion as quickly spent as any,

So too have earthly pleasures but a short stay,

Think about this, friend, and seek God's way.

Other irons were simpler. Spouses' names and their wedding date might be engraved into intertwined hearts, or perhaps a symbol like a plough, a beehive, a ship or a windmill might be used to symbolize a person's profession. The rich might have their coat of arms engraved in the metal. An iron bearing the date 1644, found on a farm, shows various farm animals, hammer, scythe and hearts.[18] Many of the engravings were quite primitive and, since most blacksmiths lacked all but the most rudimentary learning, texts which were supposed be engraved backwards as a mirror image so that they would be legible on the finished wafer, sometimes ended up with several letters back to front, unwittingly customizing a household's wafers.

Wafer and waffle recipes have remained basically unchanged since the Middle Ages. Thick waffles were made from fine wheat flour (sometimes mixed with buckwheat or rye), sugar, eggs, yeast and copious amounts of butter. Beer was the fluid of choice. The batter was left to rise before being cooked and the waffles were eaten with melted butter and sugar.[19] Wafers were generally made from a rich dough mixed with beer or cream, with flavourings like lemon zest and cinnamon. They did not always use a raising agent.[20]

The toffee-filled wafers from Gouda, *Goudse stroopwafels* (illustrated at the beginning of this chapter), have been made for more than three centuries. Although now usually bought from professionals, they were originally home-made.[21] Bakery lore suggests that they were concocted to make use of a sugar refinery by-product. They are a buttery yeast wafer which is then split and filled with an irresistible mixture of molasses, sugar, butter and spices simmered to a toffee consistency. It is the filling that is particular to Gouda; similar wafers were made in the Middle Ages, but split and eaten with melted butter.[22] The *stroopwafel* was exclusive to Gouda for a very long time, made at first only within the city, then by itinerant Gouda wafer-makers who travelled to fairs and markets around the country. In the last few decades there has been a surge of *stroopwafel* stalls, not all of which may carry the desired predicate *'Goudse'*, and almost every weekly market boasts one. Your nose – or your family – will lead you in the right direction. They are made fresh as you wait, the wafer-baker splitting the hot, delicate wafer into two perfect halves with a careless expertise born of long practice, smearing one with toffee and replacing the other in exactly the right spot. Few things are more delicious than a warm *stroopwafel* with the filling still gooey, such a far cry from its production-line supermarket counterpart. Vendors do a nice sideline in cylindrical tins and Delft Blue jars designed to hold the wafers.

Though many families still own heirloom irons as well as the stove-top versions which were popular up to the middle of the twentieth century, understandably, most people prefer to use a modern electric waffle- and wafer-maker with interchangeable plates. It takes a lot of the hard slog out of the whole process, a sobering thought when a surge of nostalgia threatens

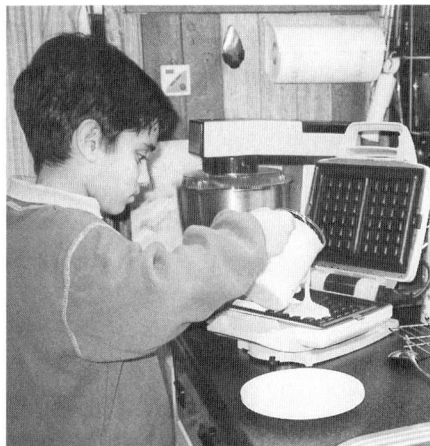

to rear its head too high. Plunging the wafer iron into the heart of a roaring fire had the benefit of drastically shortening the cooking time to mere seconds instead of the minutes needed by modern electric irons. Certainly the wafers must have had a marvellous texture. But think of the intense heat and the back-breaking work, not to mention the hit and miss affair it might be to start with, depending solely on the cook's ability to gauge the force of the fire. How much simpler, if less picturesque, modern life is.

NEW YEAR WAFER ROLLS
Nieuwjaarsrolletjes

In Zeeland the traditional New Year wafers were crisp unrolled sugar biscuits, accompanied by a glass of *stroopjannever*, gin steeped with spices and molasses.[23] Most other New Year wafers are rolled. Although the accepted Dutch word is *oublie* (from the Latin *oblatum*, the offering or the Eucharist) names vary and refer in dialect form to the various stages of preparation: *kniepertjes, kniepkoukskes* (pinched or clamped cookies, *knijpen* = to pinch), *rollechies* (little rolls, *rol* = roll), *ies'nkoek'n* (iron cookies, *ijzer* = iron) and *fluitjes* (*fluit* = flute) to list a few. They are most popular in the northern and eastern provinces where many people still make them in large quantities at home to share with friends and family. The whole process of making seemed to derive from a mixture of pagan symbolism and superstition. It was important to make them at home to propitiate the gods and demons oneself; the consistency of the batter presaged all kinds of things about the year to come. But today, the only symbolism remains the shape of the wafer, rolled up like the new year yet to unfold.

Making the wafers in the quantities deemed necessary used to be a task to tax the whole family. The kitchen fireplace might be large enough or a pit would be dug in an outhouse and a vigorous fire set to burn. Everyone had his or her own job in a surprisingly rigid hierarchy. The batter or dough would be made by the mistress helped by her elder daughters, then passed to the male head of the household, the father or eldest son or, failing them, a trusted manservant. It really was a man's job as it required great physical strength. The iron had handles more than a metre long to keep the holder a safe distance from the fire. It would be smeared with a piece of fatty bacon or a cloth dipped in rendered fat and tied to a stick. It was heated, the dough or batter poured in, clamped between the two blades, and thrust once more into the fire. It was usually the job of the smaller children to roll the wafers quickly and deftly around a dowel to form the traditional roll shape.[24]

In the recipe which follows, I have worked on the assumption that you will be using an electric waffle-maker.

Equipment: a waffle-maker fitted with wafer plates, a dowel or long-handled wooden spoon
Yield: will depend on the size, about 18–36 rolls

250g all-purpose flour	*2 eggs, well beaten*
$1/_4$ tsp salt	*250 ml milk*
200g caster sugar	*250 ml water*
75g butter, melted	

Mix the dry ingredients together in a bowl. Add the butter, egg and milk and whisk well until the batter is lump-free. Whisk in the water a little at a time. Pour the batter into a jug. Preheat the waffle-maker. Pour a little of the batter onto the hot plate and tilt the waffle-maker from side to side so that the batter flows out evenly and thinly. Close the lid. These wafers take at least five minutes to cook and the finished wafer should be speckled with lots of golden brown spots. It will be as limp as a pancake at this stage. Use a dowel or the handle of a wooden spoon to remove it and roll it immediately around this to form a multi-layered cylinder, which looks like a hastily hand-rolled beeswax candle. Eat as fresh as possible.

At the village of Geldermalsen, next-door to my home, they hold a New Year auction of fruit (mainly apples and pears). True to form, there's plenty to eat there too: all sorts of apple cakes and dumplings, and some wafers which were offered with apple on the side.

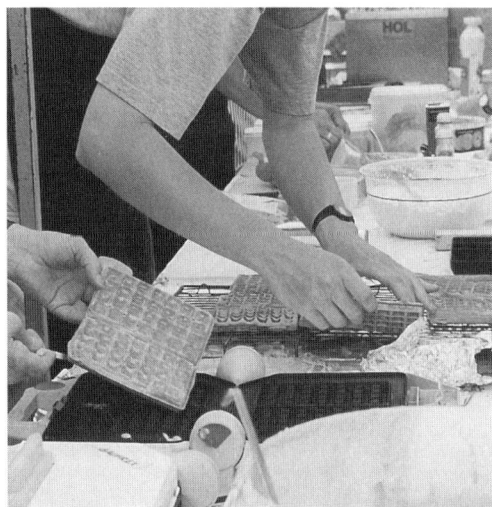

I have already mentioned (under pancakes) how a local charitable event will inevitably have its food purveyors right there, next to the jumble, poker-work and other stalls. One of my neighbours is preparing waffle batter for the stall pictured in the middle photograph. He has adapted his DIY drill to good effect. This was for the church restoration fund bring-and-buy. The photograph at the bottom is of a stall at our weekly market where John (who has been doing this since he was a boy) makes stroopwafels for sale. He has a larger griddle than would be found normally at home. The wafers are cooked between these square-meshed plates, then they are split on the board that lies next to the griddle and filled with a sugary, buttery mixture that seethes in the tub just beyond.

RYE AND MOLASSES WAFFLES FROM STAPHORST
Staphorster fleren

The *fleer* is a New Year's treat from Staphorst, a town in the north of the country, beyond Zwolle. The warm waffles are put into an airtight container to keep them limp. Left to cool on a rack they get very tough. This waffle has a flavour and texture peculiarly its own and, to be quite honest, I think it's a bit of an acquired taste. The full pungency hits you when you open the tin after a few hours to sample one. Although I refer to the *fleer* as a waffle, it is actually hard to put an exact name to it in English. It is made in a wafer iron but the finished product is not quite as thin as a wafer nor is it as thick as a waffle. *Spekkendikken*, 'bacon fatties', are made from the same batter, the difference being that bacon is cooked into the waffles. This was often eaten as a treat by the waffle-makers, made with the last bit of batter.

Equipment: a waffle-maker fitted with wafer plates
Yield: about 32 waffles, depending on the plates used

125g all-purpose flour	*100g soft dark brown sugar*
125g rye flour	*50g molasses, warmed slightly*
1 tsp ground aniseed	*2 eggs, well beaten*
¼ tsp salt	*250 ml milk, warmed*

Combine the dry ingredients in a bowl. Add the other ingredients and whisk until smooth and lump-free. Cover the bowl with a cloth and leave to stand at room temperature for one to two hours. Preheat the waffle-maker. Give the doughlike batter a good stir before making each batch. Spoon portions of the mixture onto the hot plate. Bring down the lid and cook the waffles according to the manufacturer's guidelines; an average waffle-maker will need four to five minutes. Put the waffles in an airtight tin as soon as they are cooked. Leave to cool completely in the tin before eating.

SPICED WAFFLES
Gekruide wafels

These waffles from Zeeland used to be especially in evidence at Martinmas (11 November), at the farewell meal for farm labourers hired on an annual basis. Local custom dictated that the labouring year ended at Martinmas if one served a Protestant master, or twenty days later on the feast day of St Aloysius in Catholic circles. The mistress would treat the labourers to freshly made heart-shaped waffles topped with melted butter, honey or sugar, or curd cheese made on the farm.[25] The rest of the year, it was more usual to spread the waffles with butter and sprinkle on a thick layer of brown sugar, as is still done.

Equipment: a waffle-maker with heart-shaped or rectangular plates
Yield: about 12–20 waffles, depending on the plates used

250g all-purpose flour	*1 tbsp sugar*
$^1/_2 - ^1/_4$ tsp freshly grated nutmeg	*1 egg, well beaten*
1 tsp easyblend yeast	*50g butter, melted*
$^1/_4$ tsp salt	*350 ml milk, warmed*

Combine the dry ingredients in a bowl. Add the beaten egg, butter and about half of the milk and whisk until smooth, adding the rest gradually to make a lump-free batter. Cover the bowl with a cloth and leave to stand at room temperature for one to two hours. Preheat the waffle-maker. Give the batter a good stir to deflate it and pour a ladleful into each shape. Bring down the lid and cook the waffles until they are golden brown and crisp; an average waffle-maker will need $2^1/_2 - 4$ minutes. Stack the cooked waffles on a wire rack and eat while still warm with melted butter and caster sugar, or soft brown sugar, or with curd cheese sweetened to taste.

Chapter Ten

SEASONAL BAKING

If you keep an eye on the baker's display case you will notice that, over and above what you might call a basic stock, part of the assortment varies from season to season. In spring, there are traditional Easter breads to complement the rabbits and chicks of international currency, and icing seems to be mainly yellow. During the week before 30 April the icing mysteriously changes to orange; cakes are filled with orange-flavoured creams; breads are advertised as containing lots of orange peel. The reason is patriotic. The last day of April is *Koninginnedag* – the Queen's birthday – which most of Holland celebrates by eating orange-coloured and flavoured breads and cakes. The Dutch royal dynasty is the House of Orange.

Currant loaves have become such a part of everyday life that we tend to forget that they were originally an item of great luxury, and the Easter fruit loaves of the past were much anticipated. Baked since the Middle Ages, they often referred to as *wijelbroot,* consecrated bread.[1] There are accounts of a cartload of Easter bread being baked for the household of Karel, Duke of Guelders (1467–1538) and in the sixteenth century in Amsterdam many people ordered an Easter loaf in the shape of a *Duivekater*, a beautiful festive bread, for the Saturday before Easter.[2] A recipe for Easter bread from *De Volmaakte Hollandsche Keuken-meid* (1767) advises the cook to use half a pound[3] of currants and two or three eggs to every pound of flour, along with melted butter, milk, yeast, cinnamon and nutmeg, adding that 'even candied citron won't spoil it,' a stange way of putting it, but one gets the picture of a deliciously spiced, rich fruit bread, a treat for those who could afford it.[4] Bakers often gave currant loaves at Easter and at Christmas to regular customers, a custom that died out after the First World War.[5] Some shameless souls tried to divide their custom, hoping to get more than one fruit loaf that way, but bakers had their own way of dealing with such sharp practices and usually gave a loaf that was proportionate to the money that had been spent in their shop. Up to today, few Easter breakfast or brunch tables would be complete without a rich fruit loaf of some kind.

There are still lingering traces in North and South Holland of the tradtion of eating *luilakbollen* on the Saturday before Whitsunday, a custom now obsolete in most other places. In Drenthe they were eaten on Whit Monday, in Gelderland on Ascension Day and in Groningen on Good Friday, inviting comparison with hot cross buns, both in the physical and symbolic sense. *Luilakbollen* are made from fruity, spiced dough and some versions have a cross, but this is cut into the sides of the dough so that the finished bun ends up like a four-petalled flower. Although the buns are still eaten on a small scale, often in a temporary resurgence of nostalgia, there is no longer any fringe ritual. As the tradition went, the last to rise in each each household was ribbed for his lazy habits – a *luilak* is a lazy person – and sent to the baker's to fetch the warm buns to be eaten with molasses for breakfast. As a supplement to housemates' efforts, children took great pleasure in running noisily around the streets, banging and clanging anything they had to hand and shouting at the tops of their lungs to wake up any slackers, a custom seen by folklorists as the remnant of a pagan desire to drive out the last of the winter demons.

Summer brings a lot of fruit tarts and cream cakes with fresh fruit. If the weather is especially hot, bakers replace the cream-based products with plainer and drier fare, less likely to spoil. It tends to be a slow season for most bakers unless they can count on trade from tourists.

This trade picks up with alarming briskness in late autumn when eager shopkeepers start exhorting customers to buy early for *Sinterklaas*. This is the feast of St Nicholas when, traditionally, presents are given in Holland – rather than Christmas. Bakers start preparing for the event themselves, as December is the busiest month of the year. The *Sinterklaas* season is typified by spice biscuits, and almond paste and marzipan articles.

As soon as *Sinterklaas* is over, Christmas is here. The Christmas stollen, called a *Kerststol*, is sold in prodigious quantities, while traditional specialities like *Duivekaters* and *Stevenmannen* remain limited to the happy few who know about such things. The *Duivekater* is described at the end of this chapter. *Stevenmannen* are fruit dough men, usually with a tiny clay pipe stuck into their mouths. They are a southern tradition, baked in predominantly Catholic areas where they probably originated as a speciality for the feast of St Stephen, 26 December. The stollen was supposedly introduced into Holland in the late nineteenth century by an immigrant German baker in Amsterdam.[6] As the story goes, in a fit of homesickness the baker made a beautiful stollen for his family and used it to decorate his window until they were ready to eat it. An equally homesick compatriot passed the display and couldn't believe his luck. He asked if he could buy it but the baker refused, saying it was meant for his family. One of the baker's daughters heard this and, with more business sense than her father, she suggested he sell it and bake another. And so he did, and another, and another. … The bread became all the rage and other bakers soon copied it. The last five years have seen a somewhat ludicrous rise in its popularity as we are now invited to buy stollen at other seasons, even Easter. The word is fast becoming synonymous with 'celebration bread' as marketing strategists conveniently ignore the fact that the shape of the bread symbolizes a swaddled Christchild. And entertaining though the story of the German baker may be, similar loaves called *wiggekindjes* or *wikkelkindjes* (yes, 'swaddled children') were being made in the Dutch countryside long before that baker had ever heard tell of Amsterdam.

Some once-popular December specialities have gradually disappeared. In North Holland the *Sinterklaas* treats known everywhere else in the country were often supplemented by local variants. One of these was a round currant loaf with a filling of brown sugar, cinnamon and crumbs,[7] which sounds almost identical to the *Hoornse broeder* described in the chapter on breads. More eyecatching is the *handjesame* ('hands together'), a flat light currant bun which was cut and folded to look like the intertwined fingers of two hands. It was especially popular among those who couldn't afford to give their children the more expensive *taai-taai* and *speculaas* figures,[8] but faded away in the face of plenty, yet another example of the effect prosperity can have on traditional foods. Very few people nowadays even know what a *Driekoningenbrood* is, let alone the fact that it had been immensely popular since the Middle Ages. This sweet round loaf, often decorated in the shape of a crown, was baked for Twelfth Night (as is still done in other European countries) and whoever found the dried bean baked into it was king for the evening, part of an intricate game played by a large company. The king chose a queen and lots were drawn for the other 14 roles of the royal household.[9]

December ends with a flurry of fruit doughnuts, *oliebollen*, traditionally eaten on New Year's Eve.

On the pages which follow I describe some of the more remarkable breads, cakes, biscuits or buns linked either to a specific date or festival, or to a moveable occasion such as a birthday or a village fair. An example of the latter was the *hylikmaker*, a spice shape used to couch a covert proposal of marriage. I will not, in every instance, give a recipe, but the facts alone are of sufficient interest to merit at least an account.

FAIRTIME AND COURTSHIP SPICE SHAPE
Kermiskoek *or* Hylikmaker

Het is toch zeker en gewis
Dat zonder koek geen kermis is.[10]

One thing for granted you may take,
A fair's not a fair without a [spice] cake.

Fairtime was traditionally a time to socialize, especially for those who might be stuck on inaccessible farms for most of the year, starved of company. It was also a time for young people to get a chance to meet a future partner, particularly one from outside their usual orbit. The spiced fair cake or *kermiskoek* (what is called a fairing in England) known as the *hylikmaker* was used as a subtle means of testing the water. *Hylikmaker* is a contraction of *huwelijkmaker* or marriage-maker. Folklore never tires of ascribing all kinds of admirable qualities to St Nicholas. Among several others, he is often also given the role of *huwelijksmakelaar* or marriage-broker, and this too could be contracted to *hylikmaker*. Whatever the case, the *hylikmaker* was a courtship gift, an edible love letter.

Although no overt proposal might be made, giving a girl a *hylikmaker* could have binding consequences. The girl would contrive to hold her *koek* prominently as the pair sauntered round the fairground, silently telling the world that she had an admirer. Silent is the operative word here as no speech was required during initial stages of an often intricate courtship ritual. The girl took her trophy home and her suitor had to wait in suspense until the following Sunday when he could call for coffee with the family and a clue as to where he stood. Courting etiquette varied greatly around the country and what passed for encouragement in one place might mean adamant refusal in another. In the Achterhoek, if a boy's intended sweetheart gave him a large piece of the *koek*, it meant he was welcome to press on.[11] In the Betuwe he would have to be offered the first piece, regardless of size; if he was given the last piece there was no hope.[12] In Oud Beierland to be given the crust signified refusal,[13] and in Zuid Beveland they were much more rigorous, giving back the whole thing untouched as a sign of rejection.[14] In Streefkerk, though, a girl demonstrated her refusal by eating the whole *koek* up herself.[15] That must have been particularly harsh, to lose both treat and girl in one blow! At least in some other places they were good enough to give the luckless swain the leftovers as they sent him about his business.

The inhabitants of Goes made no bones about the matter of marriage and the horse and cattle market was used unselfconsciously to exhibit more than just prime horseflesh.[16] Most young girls dreamed of being presented with a cow-shaped *koek*, decorated with her name or a verse, before the day was out. These *toondagkoeken*, exhibition cakes, are the last remnant of what used to be a widespread custom and they can still be ordered from local bakers. The other sorts that I have mentioned edged their way into the twentieth century and gradually disappeared along with a fine tradition of skill and craftsmanship.

The baking of *kermiskoeken,* among them *hylikmakers*, often ran in families. Many generations of *koek* bakers might frequent the same fairs for several decades or even centuries.[17] Fairtime was generally the only time of the year that jealously watchful local guilds permitted itinerant bakers to compete with them. It was a lucrative time for all of them as demand far oustripped supply. Those who managed to get a stall vied with each other to offer an amazing variety of delicious *koeken*. Large or small; bursting with peel or plain; hard, chewy or soft: there was something to suit every taste and pocket. They were often embellished with verses and inscriptions and while you bought a *hylikmaker* for your sweetheart, you could get *kermiskoeken* with texts and verses intended for your parents or even an old flame – which of course made it clear that she was just that. At one time it was popular for maidservants to take back a suitably humbly inscribed *koek* for their mistress.

Seventeenth- and eighteenth-century recipes for *hylikmakers* suggest a *koek* which was similar in taste and texture to *speculaas*[18] but, judging from the custom of giving crusts and end-pieces to rejected suitors, softer types of spice loaf were also used. As the Dutch word *koek* covers both eventualities it leaves enough room for speculation. Surpisingly, wheat flour seems to have been preferred to the more usual rye. Wheat flour, brown sugar, honey, potash, spices, candied citron and orange peel are kneaded and rolled out, then shaped before baking. One recipe adds that the dough may be shaped into balls but that butter and a little wine must be added. This will presuambly give a thicker and perhaps more chewy result.[19] Nowadays *koeken* are widely available and fairs no longer even sell them, having now specialized in fritters and doughnuts. People too have changed, and with them courtship patterns, so the *hylikmaker* has been consigned to folklore and nostalgia. Even if the verses were every bit as corny as those on Valentine's cards, how nice they must have been to receive to set the wordless ritual in motion.

CURRANT BREAD OR CRADLE-SHAKING BREAD FROM TWENTE

Twentse Krentenwegge *or* Kraamschudderswegge

The currant breads from Twente, in eastern Holland, are generally held to be among the best in the country. These long, flat loaves are baked for all sorts of celebrations and are usually called *Twentse krentenweggen*,[20] but by far their most traditional purpose is as a *kraamschudderswegge*. *Kraamschudden* is an expression used almost exclusively in Twente which can be roughly translated as 'cradle-shaking'.

Before the Second World War it used to be customary, especially in country districts, for relatives and neighbours to take along something edible when they visited a new baby. Often a treat for the mother would be included among the pots of soup, loaves of bread and eggs and butter. You helped each other out in times of need by making sure there was always something to offer callers and in this way even the poor could celebrate, knowing that the festivities would cost them little more than a few eggs or a roll of rusks when somebody else's time came. In Twente, the new mother's mother, sisters and neighbours came with a *kraamschudders-wegge* to welcome the baby. The system surrounding the giving of the loaves was very well regulated and the closer your relationship to the mother, the sooner you visited with your *wegge*. The size varied greatly and loaves up to two metres long were no exception. If the neighbours were giving it, the size depended on how much money had been clubbed together. The early loaves were baked free-form on the oven floor. Later, planks (propped up with bricks) were used to hold the dough in shape, so the size could be varied at will. Some bakers started to use tins after the Second World War.[21] These restricted the size, and changed the texture of the crumb as well as the soft, light side-crusts which planks insulated so effectively during baking.

As the larger loaves couldn't be taken under the arm, the baker had to be inventive with transportation. A ladder securely lashed onto a bicycle carrier was one of the most common methods, especially when it was purely a peasant tradition. As more people began to adopt it, around 1930,[22] things became quite sophisticated and the village brass band might be hired to accompany the loaf-bearers. The tradition even penetrated royal circles: a delegation of women from Twente went with their *wegge* to Soestdijk Palace in 1947 – and were cordially received by the Prince Consort – to shake the new princess's cradle.

Increasing prosperity and decreasing social control and care are gradually killing all kinds of old traditions. Fortunately, the *kraamschudderswegge* has been spared this fate, and continues to be a tangible gesture of friendship that tells its own story of a 'Dutch treat'. This and similar customs, born of generosity of spirit in the face of grinding poverty, have been robbed of their dignity in many English-speaking countries which persist in giving a slightly derogatory slant to the expressions 'going Dutch' or 'Dutch treat' (in fact, these phrases seem to be of American origin, although most of the ruder English references to the Dutch – 'Dutch comfort', 'Dutch courage' – date from the Anglo-Dutch wars of the seventeenth century). Most people don't realize that the Dutch are actually quite assiduous about treating. Seldom will a milestone pass, birth, birthday, anniversary, passing an exam or even leaving for a new job, without family, friends and colleagues being treated to cakes and pastries. Most primary schoolchildren treat their whole class at every birthday.

My husband has cousins in Twente one of whom recently had a son. When we went to visit there were two *weggen* on the kitchen table, one 18 x 75 cm, the other 14 x 50 cm, and I was assured that these were medium-sized! They were sliced and waiting to be buttered and served with tea and coffee to the visitors. Coming from outside the region, from Gelderland in the middle of the country, we were given the choice of *beschuit met muisjes* – rusks with aniseed dragées, see page 63 above – the general accompaniment to coffee on such occasions in the rest of Holland. But who on earth would miss an opportunity to eat *kraamschudderswegge* in such an authentic setting? My eyes and tastebuds, not to mention my mind, savoured every moment.

BIRTHDAYS

In Dutch, as in any other language, there are words and expressions impossible to translate accurately to convey the literal meaning and the subtle undertones. One such word is *gezellig*. It means cosy, snug, pleasant, convivial, cheerful, entertaining, welcoming and a lot more. And one expression is *naar een verjaardag gaan*. This is literally 'to go to a birthday'- not a birthday party, but a birthday. A birthday party would imply that you had received an invitation to attend and you don't really need an invitation to go to a birthday. The Dutch set great store by birthdays and it is considered a compliment if people drop in to wish you well. Birthday calendars, which often hang, inexplicably, in the lavatory, are consulted daily and busy bees will find themselves juggling the birthdays that fall on the same day. If you are the birthday girl or chap, you will have no idea of how many people will come round but in rural communities in particular, you are expected to be 'at home' to visitors. They will not take kindly to your slipping out without prior warning. If, for some reason, you can't celebrate your birthday on the actual day, it is customary to let family and friends know on which day you will be available. A birthday in Holland is *gezellig*.

The first such celebration I attended was at the house of my husband's parents, and it was a bit of a culture shock. It was my mother-in-law's birthday and the 'phone had been ringing incessantly since breakfast, conveying the good wishes of those who were unable to come. Around 10.30 in the morning, people started to arrive. Some neighbours were first. They came in, shook my mother-in-law's hand, congratulated her, then offered her a token of their esteem. Next, they shook my father-in-law's hand and congratulated him on his wife's birthday. They moved on to my husband and congratulated him on his mother's birthday. In our turn, my brother-in-law and I were also similarly congratulated. I hadn't been prepared for this. I was used to invited guests showing up at a pre-arranged time and crying or muttering, depending on their disposition, 'Happy Birthday,' before dashing off to check on the edibles. It was to get even better. More neighbours arrived and the whole ritual was repeated. When they had finished congratulating the family, they passed to the first set of neighbours and, to my great astonishment, proceeded to congratulate them on their neighbour's birthday, whereupon the wishes were reciprocated!

It was a busy morning. On arrival, the guests were given coffee with great dollops of sweetened whipped cream on top, and their choice of cake. They settled down to eat, drink and chat. These occasions are a primary source of local news and gossip and are used to compare and discuss ailments. (In one extreme case years later, I entered my living-room with fresh coffee to discover a few of my guests, socks and shoes strewn about them, displaying their bunions to each other as the rest watched interestedly proffering advice.) Meanwhile, the telephone was still ringing and trips had to be made to the railway station from time to time to collect various aunts. Each arrival was followed by the ritual handshaking and, depending on the relationship with the aunt in question, hugs and the traditional three kisses on the cheeks. Coffee and cakes made way for nibbles and drinks, and that typical Dutch celebration *bowl*. *Bowl* is a kind of very wet fruit salad – or very fruity punch, depending on how you look at it – which for some reason is always served with the drinks. It contains the maker's choice of fruit, liberally moistened with mineral water, fruit juice or white wine. It is served by the cupful and you are given a spoon – whipped cream is optional. Almost everyone had a helping. Then most of the men had a glass of gin and the women had either fruit juice or advocaat.

By midday, the first guests were ready to leave. This was accompanied by more hearty handshaking. The traditional wish of 'Many more happy and healthy years,' triggered the response, 'May you be a witness to it for many years to come.' Formalities over, they departed. The aunts were staying all day so the atmosphere was as busy as ever. Many of them only saw each other at times like this and had a lot of catching-up to do. I joined in wholeheartedly, seeing an ideal opportunity to practise my newly-learned Dutch.

The birthday I have described is an old-fashioned country celebration. Birthdays retain their importance but ways to mark them are changing. City-dwellers, or those with busy jobs, have to cope with a preordained routine, but even the busiest seldom fail to treat their colleagues to a selection of cakes at work. Children are, as ever, the lucky ones. They usually end up with two parties, one for their friends and another for relatives and adult family friends.

SEEING ABRAHAM

Men celebrating their fiftieth birthday are often presented with an Abraham cake. Its overt biblical link can be found in St John 8:57 where Jesus is asked, 'And you who are not yet fifty have already seen Abraham?' suggesting that at 50 a person has reached one of the highest points of his life and has achieved a certain level of wisdom. Nowadays, as gender equivalence takes root, women may be given their 'Sara' – she was, of course, the wife of Abraham.

The custom of giving a cake originated in North Holland and has now spread all over the country. Most bakers have their own special way of making an Abraham and 'secret' recipes abound. The first were made from bread dough, often enriched with dried fruit. Nowadays they can be made of almost any bakery ingredients: cake batter, *speculaas* dough, rich bread dough, *boterkoek* dough or even chocolate. The bakers who use *speculaas* dough often cheat a little by using a St Nicholas mould since Abraham, like St Nicholas, is bearded and wears a robe. These Abrahams are usually crisp and biscuit-like. Other bakers use a metal strip moulded into a suitable shape, particularly useful for confining rich buttery doughs. The Abrahams made from yeast dough are usually free-form but are layered and sculpted to give an extra dimension. Cake-batter Abrahams are either baked in the right shape or, more often than not, simply cut into shape from a slab of sponge. A filling is often baked into the other kinds of Abraham, usually almond paste or dried fruit or even a deliciously spiced and spiked combination of the two. Whatever they are made of, they are decorated with

A house decorated to celebrate the owner's fiftieth birthday. The little flags are printed with the legend 'Abraham 50' and the effigy suggests that the birthday-boy is a football fan.

combinations of whipped cream, marzipan, icing, fruit and nuts to bring out the features. A verse often decorates the cake, like the following trenchant but no doubt kindly meant example:

Wees over de eerste 50 jaar niet verwonderd,
U mag dat zijn als u bent honderd.[23]

Don't let yourself be amazed by the first 50 years,
Time enough for that when you're 100.

The Dutch birthday mood is very much in evidence at a fiftieth birthday and cake is only part of the celebration. Where I live, a life-sized dummy is secretly made and dressed in the clothes of the man it represents. Wherever possible a salient physical feature is teasingly emphasized. The dummy is propped up outside the front door surrounded by bunting and banners announcing the event. It isn't at all strange to find messages like 'So-and-so has seen Abraham. Hoot three times!' People, even complete strangers, comply, entering wholeheartedly into the spirit of things. The computer age has brought a new element. Relatives and friends print out posters, complete with photograph, and stick them on any handy trees and lampposts. A fiftieth birthday, especially in the countryside, is not some-thing you can keep quiet – often quite literally. Many an 'Abraham' has been jolted awake at the crack of dawn by an awful, enthusiastic cacophony as well-wishers gather under his window with pots, pans, lids and spoons. Those souls blessed with clear consciences experience only a momentary irritation which flees as they remember what day it is. Those burdened with some degree of guilt can teeter on the brink of trauma for a few suspenseful seconds. An acquaintance of ours had gone to bed on the eve of his fiftieth birthday wrestling with his feelings as he had made an unpopular decision in his capacity as club president. When he was startled awake next morning by sounds he couldn't quite place, his first thought was that a lynch mob had come to get him!

PALM SUNDAY BREAD FIGURES
Palmpaasjes

Palm Sunday *Palmpasen* processions commemorating Jesus' triumphant entry into Jerusalem have been held in Holland for at least four centuries. Like so many customs, pagan and Christian elements have become so inter-twined that it is impossible to isolate them. The green branches and twigs, for instance, represent both olive and palm branches as well as the earlier May tree, a fertility symbol. From the mid-sixteenth century it was customary for children as well as adults to go door to door with green branches asking for money, bread and eggs.[24] They hung whatever they were given in the branches and, after the custom of begging had died out, the decorative tradition remained. Bread figures and other refinements, generally edible, were integrated into the greenery.

By the eighteenth century ready-made *Palmpaasjes* could be bought in the cities, as is depicted in more than one painting and etching.[25] Those who had access to greenery used pine or other evergreen branches and decorated them according to regional traditions. The two main types were the Frisian and Saxon.[26] The Frisian type was popular not only in Friesland, but also in North and South Holland and in Utrecht. A long stick was used to make a composition of greenery, fruit and baked goods, rather like a Christmas tree in miniature. Instead of the star there was a bread bird on top, usually a swan. In Alkmaar, a pair of swans with their tails touching were used. The bird was often the gift of a baker to his regulars. He might make 500 or 600 figures, giving away the smaller ones as encouragement to buy the larger.[27] This bird was for many children the edible climax to the day's festivities, apparent in one of the songs they sang during the procession.[28]

Hoantien op 'n stokkien	*Rooster on a stick up there*
Mit zien roodbont rokkien,	*Dressed up in the red you wear,*
Hoantien mit zien linkerpoot,	*So my left-legged friend,*
Vanoavend is mien hoantien dood.	*Tonight will see your end.*

Strings of nuts and dried fruit like figs were twined into the greenery along with currant buns, slices of spice loaf and pretzel biscuits. In the eighteenth century, coloured eggs became popular. The Saxon type of *Palmpaasje* used a plaited bread wreath as a basis. It was generally round, though square ones were not unknown. Dough spokes would be put in (in the case of the rectangular ones, a cross), and swan figures were placed in the empty spaces. It was usually mounted on a stick fitted with a horizontal wooden cross to support it. If it was to be used vertically, it would be mounted against a sturdy branch. Decorations were similar to the Frisian type. The horizontal ones look rather like well-stocked bird-feeding tables, complete with birds.

Palmpasen processions were quite popular and matter-of-course up to the first half of the twentieth century but gradually appeared to peter out. They are now regaining popularity as various organizations, from schools to local councils,[29] awaken to the growing need to make an effort to preserve tradition. At our village Sunday School the children make bread figures and assemble their own *Palmpaasje*, but there is no procession. In the villages and towns where there are processions, they are often accompanied by local brass bands which now take the place of the simple traditional songs that used to be sung, songs which often had a liturgical basis and folkloric elements, which none but the oldest generation remembers. People complain that the spontaneity of the occasion is lost when artificial means are used to keep the tradition alive, but is this not a question of cultural evolution? Traditions may, and sometimes must, evolve to stay alive, and it is not always a negative development. The heartening thing is that the bakery links remain strong. Few know that the bird is meant to be a swan whose origins lie in Nordic mythology, or that the bread wheel symbolizes the eternity of life. The swan may be called a chick or a hen and may even be made in the shape of a rooster, and the wheel may be just a wreath; what remains unchanged is that they are made of bread.

THE FEAST OF ST NICHOLAS
Sinterklaas

The fifth of December in Holland is as fraught with excitement as Christmas Eve in most other parts of the world. It is the eve of the feast of St Nicholas of Myra and both saint and feast are affectionately referred to as *Sinterklaas*. Children have another name for the evening of 5 December – *pakjesavond* – literally 'parcel evening'. They look forward to being showered with presents. The feast has been celebrated in Holland since the twelfth century.[30] St Nicholas was born in southern Turkey and rose to be Bishop of Myra, now Demre. He died on 6 December AD 324 and it is the anniversary of his death, strangely enough, which is commemorated. He was a man of good deeds, some of them sounding suspiciously like miracles. One of the most popular legends is that he saved a devil from Hell, and the grateful devil became his first familiar or helper, *Zwarte Piet* or Black Peter, although Zwarte Piet didn't appear on the scene in the flesh until the mid-nineteenth century.[31] This figure of a jet-black servant speaking broken Dutch and unashamedly displaying ignorance at every turn has, unsurprisingly, caused offence in former Dutch colonies like Surinam where the custom was promptly abolished on independence in 1975, to be reinstated in 1992.[32] In Holland few such qualms exist; even the normally vociferous human-rights and equal-opportunities groups keep quiet long enough for everyone to enjoy the festivities unburdened by worry of correction. Most people console themselves by the thought that the colour of Zwarte Piet's skin is caused by soot from hell-fire, or creeping up and down chimneys as he drops off presents, rather than from natural pigmentation. Of course, for such an important mission as distributing presents and toys, one assistant is never enough, so the good saint is accompanied by an army of blackamoors. The Pieten are loved for their tricks and antics and St Nicholas would never be able to put on as good a show by himself.

Sinterklaas and his two Zwarte Pieten (Black Peters) stride through the village after visiting a children's party. In another part of the street, shoes are placed near the chimney to receive his largesse.

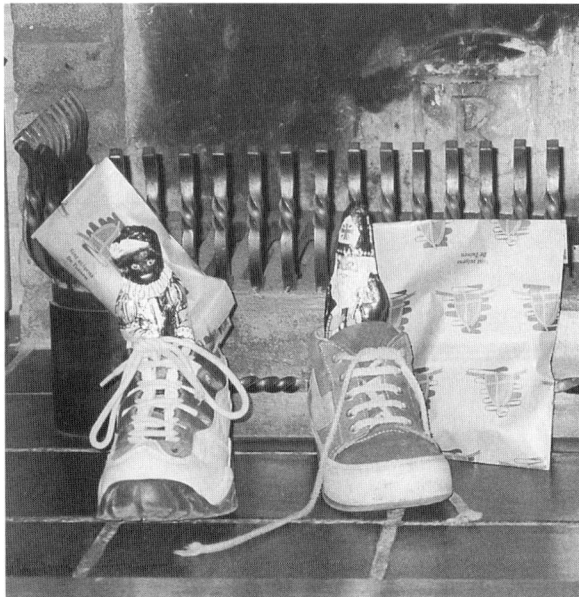

Somewhere along the way Myra became Mila, the devil became a Moor and instead of coming from Turkey, Sinterklaas now comes from Spain. The devil and Moor certainly appeal more to children than the folklorists' interpretation of the Pieten as darker forces of the inevitable midwinter theme.

There is now ritual and performance surrounding the arrival of Sinterklaas (putatively on a boat from Spain) in Holland each year. This takes place around the middle of November and is broadcast live on national television. A different town is chosen as host and landfall to his barque. The mayor waits as patiently as he can on the quay amidst mounting excitement. From the time the steamship bearing St Nicholas glides into sight, the Pieten on board begin their capers that charm all but the most cynical. The Head Piet and the Directions Piet invariably manage to 'lose the way' and must be gently upbraided by their master. When the boat docks it disgorges a stately white-bearded figure in red velvet with gold trimming and white lace, with the mitre of his office on his aged locks. In one hand he has a staff and in the other his Red Book in which the behaviour of each Dutch child is recorded. His Pieten, in doublet and pantaloons, mill around him, blackened faces contrasting sharply with pristine ruffs. Most carry jute sacks filled with *pepernoten* and sweets which are strewn with great abandon, some landing in expectantly outstretched hands, the rest trampled underfoot. St Nicholas mounts his white horse, Amerigo, and sets off on his social round through Holland. Once he has officially 'arrived' he can visit other towns and villages and his Pieten are well known for leaving black handprints all over primary schools, sometimes even handfuls of hay and the odd carrot rejected by Amerigo, as they hide sweets and biscuits in the children's desks during the night.

Bakers await St Nicholas' arrival as eagerly as the children. It marks the onset of their busiest season, which can generate as much as a third of their annual profit. Typical Sinterklaas specialities like *speculaas, pepernoten, banketstaven, taai-taai* and chocolate initials are sold in prodigious quantities, as is marzipan in various forms. Every bakery, and nowadays even the bakery departments of supermarkets, has a huge pink marzipan pig on the counter and you can buy pieces of trotter or snout or whatever takes your fancy by weight. Today, the local baker supplies your needs but, from the sixteenth century up to the mid-nineteenth century, St Nicholas markets were popular in Holland, especially in Amsterdam where he is patron saint.[33] In addition to toys and gifts, the stalls were crammed with all sorts of edible Sinterklaas specialities which have remained more or less unchanged over the centuries.

Children start lobbying for extra shoe-setting days. Traditionally, they put a clog or shoe filled with hay or a carrot for Amerigo by the fireplace, hoping to be rewarded. The climax is reached on the evening of 5 December, when Sinterklaas and his helpers deposit a jute sack filled with presents on almost every doorstep. Neighbours are generally charged with this task and they thump enthusiastically on doors and windows in true Piet-like manner. If that is too ordinary you can always rent a Sinterklaas and a few Pieten. The sack usually contains 'surprises', presents packed in ingenious home-made containers – looking like anything from steamships to doll's houses, clocks and cars – usually reflecting in some way the recipient. I admit to being the television and toffee type – they are so easy to make from shoe boxes. The surprise is accompanied by doggerel designed to tease as much as possible and give deliberately misleading, but not untrue hints about the contents. One Sinterklaas years ago, a present to me from my husband was a little box accompanied by a lengthy verse replete with allusions to riches, gold and far-off lands. Imagine my initial chagrin when what I expected – or hoped – to be a piece of exotic jewellery turned out to be a box of saffron strands. Yet there wasn't an untrue word in the whole verse. It's great fun as you read out the verses to each other and it allows you to be sneakingly didactic with the children.

Commerce beckons and, under the influence of Santa Claus, satellite television and Christmas, more emphasis is being placed on the presents and their value. Some people, especially those without children, now prefer to have Santa put their verse-free presents under the Christmas tree. This trend is a bitter irony, for we are now reimporting a commercialized version of our own St Nicholas. Santa Claus came into being in the 1820s in the United States, the brainchild of Clement Clark Moore, a respected professor of languages at a New York seminary and author of *The Night before Christmas*.[34] St Nicholas was undoubtedly role model (particularly as his rebirth was in a town once known as New Amsterdam), recognizable in spite of the addition of other elements. By the time a well-known American soft drinks company decided to use 'Santa Claus' in an advertising campaign the course was set. Personalities are shaped by cultures and there is a world of difference between the stately and gentle old cleric and the ebullient man bellowing 'ho ho ho'. It would be a great pity to see St Nicholas succumb now after weathering so many storms. Under pressure from the clergy, lawmakers during the Reformation went as far as banning St Nicholas markets and open festivities, as in Delft in 1600, but it had little actual effect apart from provoking a spirit of rebellion. More than anything, St Nicholas personifies the spirit of the season in Holland. His tacit secularization over the centuries has helped keep him alive. He belongs to the nation as a whole rather than to any church faction. His remains may lie in Bari, taken there by Italian sailors at the beginning of the eleventh century, and he may be the patron saint of sailors and young girls among others, but nobody loves him more than Dutch children – even the ones who claim to no longer 'believe in Sinterklaas'. And such is the respect he commands that it is still not the done thing to start making Christmas preparations, or even put up decorations, before St Nicholas has left again for Spain.

SPICE NUTS or PEPPERNUTS
Kruidnootjes *or* Pepernoten

Spice nuts have always been associated with Sinterklaas and you will find them equally in a Jan Steen painting of St Nicholas Eve or in the eager hands and mouths of modern Dutch children. These small spicy biscuits taste best when Zwarte Pieten grab them by the handful from their jute sacks and scatter them indiscriminately. They are mixed with small fruit-flavoured sweets for this purpose and the combination is called *strooigoed* or strewing-stuff. *Pepernoten* remained as they had been for centuries until all of a sudden, about three or four years ago, a manufacturer decided to dip them in chocolate and a fabulousy simple but novel combination was born. This seems to have sparked off a whole new trend and in the Sinterklaas season you will find the spice nuts in breads, cakes and puddings, much as *bitterkoekjes* or macaroons are used the rest of the year. Most of the combinations work very well, but some can be studies in overreach. This year a leading supermarket chain combined the whole Sinterklaas season in one tart. The base was made from *speculaas* and the almond-paste filling was topped with spice nuts. I don't think it was much of a success, at least not in my area.

Although most *pepernoten* are manufactured commercially, there are still subtle regional differences. Frisians like a lot of aniseed in their dough. In Zeeland the spice nuts are made from a light-coloured dough also flavoured liberally with aniseed. Instead of being shaped into balls the dough is rolled out and cut into chunks which are often dipped into aniseed-flavoured flour before being baked.

The recipe I give here is for the popular type which is usually mass-produced and sold all over the country. They are very easy to make – child's play, really. My nine-year-old son has made them from scratch to help me test this recipe. When my daughter was five, her class made several batches and I vividly remember how proud she was of her efforts, many of which looked like rabbit droppings. That is the only thing you have to watch out for here, but rolling fairly uniform balls will make the end-product please both eye and palate.

Oven: 180°C ♦ Tin: 2 baking sheets ♦ Time: about 17 minutes
Yield: about 128 spice nuts

100g butter, softened
125g soft dark brown sugar
250g all-purpose flour
2 tsp baking powder
¼ tsp salt
Spice mix: 1 ½ tsp ground cinnamon, ½ tsp ground ginger,
½ tsp ground cardamom, ¼ tsp ground mace, ¼ tsp ground cloves
2 tbsp molasses
4 tbsp milk

Beat the butter and sugar until smooth. Add the other ingredients and knead well. Shape into a ball, cover and chill for about an hour. Roll 128 hazelnut-sized balls from the dough. The easiest way to do this is to divide the dough into quarters and then divide each quarter into 32 pieces. Space them evenly on the baking sheets. Bake one sheet at a time for about 17 to 20 minutes. They must be quite hard when they have cooled. Cool on a wire rack and store in an airtight container.

The array of spices (kruiden) available at a market stall, including mixtures suitable for baking such as rommelkruid *and* speculaas *mix.*

CHEWY ANISEED SLABS
Taai-taai

Taai-taai is one of the oldest kinds of spice cake, actually an ancestor of *speculaas*, but both manage to coexist in perfect harmony. It is sometimes shaped in a mould but it won't give the sharp contours of *speculaas* and is very chewy in texture – *taai* means tough. Unlike other types of spice cake you will rarely find it except in the Sinterklaas season. Some bakers start making their *taai-taai* dough months in advance to allow it to ripen properly – many have been known to start at the end of the summer, which has the added benefit of being the quietest time in the bakery.

Oven: 220°C ◆ Tin: 2 sheets, lined with baking parchment
Time: about 7 minutes ◆ Yield: 32

First day:
250g rye flour
250g all-purpose flour
250g honey
250g molasses
50g water

Second day:
1 $^1/_2$ tsp ground cinnamon
1 $^1/_2$ tsp ground aniseed
$^1/_2$ tsp ground ginger
$^1/_4$ tsp freshly grated nutmeg
2 $^1/_4$ tsp bicarbonate of soda

Glaze:
beaten egg

First day:
Mix the flours and set aside. Put the honey, molasses and water in a sauce-pan over low heat. Let it come to the boil, stirring from time to time. Cool slightly then pour it over the flour and knead to a dough. Shape into a ball and leave to cool completely. Cover and set aside in a cool place for 24 hours.

Second day:
Knead the spices and bicarbonate of soda into the ripened dough. Knead thoroughly so that everything is well incorporated and there are no more white streaks or lumps. Turn the dough out onto a floured surface and roll out to a rectangle of 28 x 40 cm. Cut into smaller rectangles of 5 x 7 cm and space evenly on the baking sheets. Brush with beaten egg and bake for about 7 minutes. Cool on a wire rack. Store in an airtight container for 24 hours before eating to allow the flavours to mature. They will keep for several weeks.

The topmost photograph is of rollers used to produce speculaas *biscuits in a bakery. The sort of result intended is pictured in the two photographs below.*

162

SPECULAAS SPICE BISCUITS

It is not quite clear whether the word *speculaas* takes its name from *speculum* or *speculator*; there is something to be said for both. *Speculum* means mirror and the biscuit you get from the mould is the mirror image of the mould itself. *Speculator* means 'he who sees all', in this case St Nicholas of Myra. One wildly incredible story suggests that it comes from *speculatie*, speculation, and that it was first baked as a gamble by an enterprising baker. Whatever the actual origin of the word, this biscuit is one of the most typical of Sinterklaas specialities. Supermarkets stock the basic kind prepackaged all year round but in December whole streets are perfumed with the enticing aroma of spices as bakers take yet another freshly baked batch of *speculaas* from the oven. They can be filled with almond paste or be plain; thick or thin; cakelike or crisp; roughly shaped in chunks or beautifully moulded into biscuits. The moulded biscuits have been made for many centuries. Nowadays most are shaped mechanically, as individual moulding takes a lot of time. Before machines became widespread, at the beginning of the twentieth century, *speculaas* bore testimony to professional skill and craftsmanship, not only those of the baker, but of the carver who had transformed an inanimate lump of wood into an evocative work of art.

The moulds were sometimes carved by the bakers themselves in their spare time. More often than not they were bought or commissioned from travelling carvers. Some examples of these moulds are used as ornaments to the beginning of each chapter in this book. Pear, pitch pine and ash were the favoured woods, although beech was preferred for larger moulds. The subject was the choice of either carver or buyer and despite the attempts of St Eligius in the seventh century – he was apostle of the Belgians and Frisians, known also as St Eloi – to ban the carving of deer, women and erotic scenes, and later those of the Church to forbid what was construed to be a form of idolatry, a stunning diversity remained. Most of the moulds which have survived now reside on museum shelves. They may gaze woodenly at the casual beholder but the discerning eye will see social history unfold as Biblical figures like Adam and Eve, Jonah and the whale, King David with his harp and angels in various postures rub shoulders with Napoleon, William of Orange, soldiers and horsemen. A slim sword bears the legible and heartening text *Deese saabel is gesont en maakt geen wont*, literally 'This sword is healthy and makes no wound', a reminder of the medicinal properties claimed for spice cakes and biscuits, sold by apothecaries in the distant past. Ships were a favourite theme, from rowing boats to sailboats and caravels, and fish and mermaids were not forgotten. Stagecoaches and carriages made way for steam engines and bicycles.

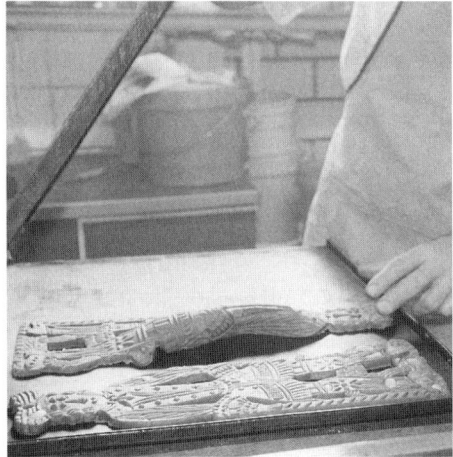

Mr Spil at the Bakery Museum at Medemblik cranks out speculaas *biscuits using the rollers pictured on page 162. In the lower photographs, he is making a much larger biscuit, the wooden mould for which is seen on the left.*

164

Knife grinders, organ grinders, coopers, milkmaids, spinners, shepherds and butchers are just a few of the occupations captured in wood, along with various animals, farm wagons and even a wheelbarrow carrying a trussed pig. Our ancestors' happy moments can be relived in the portrayals of babies in ornate or wicker cradles; lovers on bended knee wooing simpering maidens; as well as the smug-looking couples they later became. Closer scrutiny reveals a great deal of symbolism: mermaids and mermen are mythological incarnations of various gods; spinners spin the thread of life; an innocuous-looking apple tree could be the tree of life; ships a memory of the pagan death ships; animals tell of gruesome sacrifice. It is interesting to reflect that the spicy morsels popped into our eager mouths are substitutes for those animals sacrificed to natural forces and that present-day December festivities are firmly rooted in pagan midwinter customs.

The moulds were carved with amazing clarity and every detail was visible on the finished figure, which could be from a few centimetres to a metre high. The completed biscuit was often enhanced by gilding. The Dutch author Hildebrand sketches a charming scene in his *Camera Obscura* (1839) of a group of friends pleasurably engaged in gilding baker de Groot's figures in his living room, chatting as they use fine brushes and a rabbit's tail to highlight delicate details, being careful to use just enough water – too little would allow the gilding to loosen easily and too much would make it dull. There was a price to pay for all this beauty. The dough had to be hard enough to show all the details of the mould thus to deserve gilding. This type of dough is not made any more. What we have lost in aesthetic pleasure we have certainly gained in flavour. *Speculaas* has become less hard and far more buttery. Most household shops sell moulds today. Though they are mass-produced and usually limited to ships, windmills, Zwarte Piet and St Nicholas, they turn out quite attractive biscuits. Success, however, greatly depends on the mould being well seasoned. This can be achieved only by repeated use.

MY MOTHER-IN-LAW'S
BUTTERY SPECULAAS

My mother-in-law loved cakes and pastries and always had a supply of home-baked treats on hand which were hospitably pressed on even the most chance visitor. She disliked fussy, messy baking and over the years she perfected a few foolproof recipes. Her secret ingredient was butter, lots of it, and she could never understand why people could bother to waste their time with margarine. She loved to see people eat well and anyone doing odd jobs in the house would be called to table regularly for generous helpings of cakes and biscuits washed down with strong coffee, with hot frothing milk that had still been inside a cow that morning. Notoriously unreliable plumbers and carpenters were known to turn up on time for her and I'm quite sure that it was no coincidence that they tended to arrive around coffee time for even the smallest of jobs. This *speculaas* was never around for long enough to get stale and was eaten straight from the baking tin more often than not.

Oven: 180°C ♦ Time: about 30 minutes
Tin: sheet 25 x 35 cm or similar dimensions, well buttered

250g all-purpose flour
175g butter, chilled and cubed
200g soft dark brown sugar
$^1/_8$ tsp salt
$^1/_2$ tsp baking powder
Spice mixture: 1 $^1/_2$ tsp ground cinnamon, $^1/_2$ tsp ground cardamom,
$^1/_4$ tsp ground ginger, $^1/_4$ tsp ground aniseed, $^1/_4$ tsp ground cloves,
$^1/_8$ tsp freshly grated nutmeg, $^1/_8$ tsp ground mace
1 egg, beaten
75g sliced almonds

Rub the butter into the flour with your fingertips to a texture of fine bread-crumbs. Add the sugar, salt, baking powder and spices and mix well. Add the egg and knead lightly to a smooth dough. Press this dough evenly onto the baking sheet and scatter the almonds on top. Bake for about 30 minutes. Cool to lukewarm in the tin. Cut into squares for serving and cool comp-letely on a wire rack. Store in an airtight tin.

ALMOND-PASTE PASTRY STAFF AND LETTERS
Banketstaaf *and* Banketletters

Pastry staffs and letters filled with almond paste are a Sinterklaas speciality. The staff, just a straight and simple affair, represents the elegantly curved bishop's crozier carried by St Nicholas. Letters represent one's initials. Theoretically you can buy any letter you like though 'S' and 'M' are the ones most likely to be found. Even if your letter is not in stock most bakers will cheerfully take your order and produce one to your specifications. Nowadays the letters are free-form but in a few of Clara Peeters' early seventeenth-century still-lifes, there are beautifully fashioned pastry letters whose meticulous detailing suggests that they were baked in a mould. From the way the pastry is folded at the ends, it seems fair to surmise that they contained a filling of some kind, perhaps the same almond paste used today. These were not the only letters baked in those days. Peeters' contemporary Peter Binoit painted a still-life with light and dark letter shapes as the main component. The type of ridging on the letters indicates very strongly that they were made from *taai-taai*-like dough flavoured in two ways, pressed into moulds and then baked on a sheet. A recipe from 1750 shows how little the preparation of the *staaf* has changed over the centuries.[35] Equal quantities of almonds and sugar are pounded with egg and lemon zest and the mixture is used to fill pastry, either shaped into long tubes or modelled into letters of the maker's choice. A minor difference with modern methods is that the pastry is slit in a few places, exposing some of the filling, perhaps a decorative element or simply a practical measure to prevent pent-up steam from splitting the seams as it bakes.

The fascination with letters at Sinterklaas goes back several centuries. St Nicholas appears in this context as patron saint of literacy. People of the middling sort in the nineteenth century habitually covered the children's Sinterklaas gifts with a sheet and put a bread-dough initial on each pile to indicate ownership.[36] Children at convent schools in the Middle Ages were taught their letters using bread-dough examples, which they were allowed to eat as a reward.[37] Eating letters was supposed to confer knowledge on those who lacked learning, and there are old tales of well-meaning mothers who cut up paper letters into their children's porridge to speed up the learning process.[38] Up to today, the expression 'to eat letters' is a synonym for acquiring knowledge. Letters and Sinterklaas are still closely linked but the letters have become for the greater part chocolate. This trend started about a century ago. In the weeks leading up to Sinterklaas more than twenty million letters are sold – not bad for a country with a population of just over fifteen million.[39] You can buy them in several flavours of chocolate and varying size and even LCD digital letters are made. Shortly after Sinterklaas, the unsold letters are returned to the factory to be melted down – they are for that season only. Pastry letters and staffs can't be recycled in this way but after 5 December the shape is changed to a circle and the same ingredients produce Christmas wreaths.

SHINBONE BREAD
Duivekater

The *duivekater* is a speciality of the province of North Holland, especially the Zaandam area. It is in general a delicately and subtly flavoured sweet bread, but some versions call for currant dough. One of its characteristic features is the shinbone shape: a long cylinder with knobs at either end, a reminder of its origins. In pagan times whole animals would be sacrificed to propitiate gods and evil spirits. For instance, they would be offered up and buried in a field as safeguard against damage to crops. Eventually, instead of whole animals, limbs were used, like shinbones, and these were gradually replaced by baked offerings in the form of sweet breads. Judging from its name, the *duivekater* may have replaced a sacrificial cat.[40] *Duive(ls)kater* means 'Devil's tomcat'. This is certainly more plausible than the other popular explanation which is that the name is derived from *deux fois quatre*.[41] When the Huguenots fled to Holland from France they are said to have brought many fine breads with them and *deux fois quatre* supposedly refers to the price of one of these. It's a nice story but it lacks basis. Although the majority of *duivekaters* look like shinbones, there are variants: diamonds, the odd round one, and even a loaf made like a hedgehog by clipping the sides of an elongated piece of dough in several places.[42]

As in so many other cases, pagan midwinter customs were transposed to Christmas, and the *duivekater* became a December speciality. It is difficult to say precisely when the tradition of making *duivekaters* in their present form started. Large white festive breads had been popular since the Middle Ages, as a fifteenth-century decree testifies. It forbade bakers in Zwolle to make large, costly white loaves except at Easter and midwinter.[43] The *duivekater* was certainly very much in evidence in the seventeenth century, and it had very likely become synonymous with a midwinter gift in a few cases.[44] In Jan Steen's painting of St Nicholas' Eve an intricate *duivekater* has a place of prominence in the foreground. In his painting of the Leiden baker Arend Oostwaard and his wife there is also a *duivekater* on display among their wares. The latter has shinbone knobs but the former is a stylized diamond shape without knobs. The cuts are very intricate and this kind of cut became known among bakers as the 'Jan Steen cut'.

A culinary encyclopedia of 1957 not only gives a recipe for a sweet, lemon-flavoured *duivekater*, there are step-by-step photographs showing how to shape it, as well as of the finished product.[45] By the third edition, 1982, the recipe remains as a kind of curiosity but the photographs have disappeared. The *duivekater* is losing ground, perhaps because of the time needed to shape and decorate it, but in the Zaandam area you can buy *duive-katers* all year round. How do the bakers manage it? Very simply: most bake it in a tin and make a series of cuts on the crust which is the only thing it has in common with its ancestor. A few bakers in other places have picked up on the idea, and while it's good to see the bread getting some well-deserved attention, it is unfortunate that its identity is fading. What is particularly distressing is that there is a native loaf in the Zaandam area called the *Zaanse snijder* which has a series of parallel cuts on the top and it is similar to the modern baker's version of the *duivekater*. One can only hope that complete assimilation never takes place. The loaf is very attractive in its simplicity but bears little resemblance to its distinguished forebear.

There are a few other bread types which are related to the *duivekater*, either through a similarity in shape or in origin, and they all seem to echo the midwinter theme. The *kossewaegens* or *Kerstwiggen* (*Kerst* is Christmas) of Zeeland are made from a rich fruity dough and have a shin-bone shape. Smaller *Kersttimpen* are shaped from an elongated piece of dough which is snipped at either end before baking. Vestiges of sacrificial offering remain in the *kruidbroodjes* which are made in Rotterdam during December. These elliptical rolls are flavoured with finely chopped citron and have a reddish tinge. The colour, perhaps once given by blood, is now generally imparted by cherry juice or in a few cases, *rommelkruid*, 'mixed spices' [*rommel* means literally 'junk' or 'mess'; *kruid* is the Dutch for spice], that is used to flavour sweet and savoury dishes alike.

NEW YEAR'S EVE DOUGHNUTS
Oliebollen

New Year's Eve sees a plate – or bucket – of *oliebollen* (literally 'oil balls') in almost every Dutch house. Even the most chic party has them, as do all the live television chat shows and cabaret programmes. On the following day there lingers all over Holland the smell of stale oil mixed with the gunpowder from the fireworks and squibs which were used to greet the new year. Those who don't make their own, from scratch or with packaged mix, can buy them from the baker or supermarket. In many towns, there is often the same elaborately decorated and painted van, resplendent with shimmering chandeliers, which goes to local fairs, the only other time of the year *oliebollen* are eaten. This itinerant vending is not new. In former centuries cities bristled with *oliekoek* stands and they were eaten in large quantities at home, and at inns too,[46] all year round. *Oliebollen* appear to date from around the sixteenth century, when they were made in wealthy households. Jan ter Gouw gives a palpably nostalgic description of a female vendor in the mid-nineteenth century: when he was young, she was fat, cheerful and prosperous, unlike her poor, lean and languishing counter-part when he came to write his account of folk life in the 1870s. As she fried, she sang:

> Zie, jonge Heer, wat zijn ze bol
> Ze zijn gelijk een stuivers knol.
> Ook heb ik Koekebakjes,
> Zo asje wil met kaas of spek.
> Kom, lieve, kleine lekkerbek!
> Wagt nou maar niet tot strakjes!

> *See, young sir, how they are round*
> *Like an enormous turnip from the ground.*
> *I have little cakes too,*
> *With cheese or bacon if you like them that way.*
> *Come, dear little gourmet!*
> *Don't wait until later, will you!*

Mid-nineteenth-century recipes for *oliekoeken* are almost identical to modern ones. A thick batter is made from flour, milk, currants, raisins, peel, apples, nuts and eggs, then fried in a mixture of lard and rapeseed oil.[47] Nowadays most people use a neutral-tasting oil, but a southern version of the *oliebol*, the *smoutebol* (*smout* = lard) is still fried in lard. Little can compare with a home-made *oliebol*, eaten while it is still warm. In our house my husband is the *oliebol*-maker, a tradition he took over when his mother died. She used to make several buckets-full because you never knew who might drop in, a tendency I have had to curb in my husband, especcially as he gets rather offended if we don't start queueing up as soon as the first ones come out of the oil – and stay there to taste each subsequent batch. I can never forget that when I went into labour on the night of 2 January, it took me some time to realize what was really happening – my first instinct was to blame the queer feeling inside me on a surfeit of *oliebollen*.

The American doughnut has its roots in the Dutch *oliekoek*. It appears to have had two points of entry: the Pilgrims had learned to make them in Holland, where they had stayed from 1607 to 1620, so took them to New England.[48] In addition, the seventeenth-century Dutch settlers of New Amsterdam made them regularly. Washington Irving, ceaselessly poking fun at the Dutch settlers, is nevertheless compelled to remark favourably at least twice on their 'olykoeks'. In *The History of New York...by Diederich Knickerbocker* he mentions that the table of the Dutch settlers was 'always sure to boast an enormous dish of balls of sweetened dough, fried in hog's fat, and called doughnuts or olykoeks – a delicious kind of cake, at present scarce known in the city, excepting in genuine Dutch families.'[49] In *The*

A mobile oliebol *stall of giant proportions. The interiors of these trailers are decorated like an old-fashioned domestic kitchen. Flanking the sales counter is a picture of baker blowing his horn, a modern rendering of the traditional portrayal of bakers – compare it to that reproduced on the cover of this book.*

Making oliebollen *for the New Year. My neighbour produces enormous quantities of them. So many, indeed, that he retreats into his workshop to undertake the cooking for fear the smell of oil will permeate the house. For friends and neighbours, he also makes apple beignets, pictured third from the top. The bottom photo-graph is of a fine tray of* oliebollen *.*

172

Legend of Sleepy Hollow he describes the 'ample charms of the Dutch country tea-table', in a passage which is an ode to Dutch baking and the skill of Dutch housewives: the groaning table offered room to an abundance of good things, among them 'the doughty doughnut, the tenderer olykoek, and the crisp and crumbling cruller,[50] sweet cakes and short cakes, ginger cakes and honey cakes, and the whole family of cakes.'[51]

How the American doughnut got its hole is another story, destined to remain perpetually shrouded in legend. Though I can't vouch for its authenticity, I won't keep this little nugget from you: it is popularly believed in Dutch baking circles that at some point the *oliebol* taken to America by the first Dutch settlers refused to cook through, so an enterprising pioneer fryer decided to make a hole in the centre. As a theory it has about as much going for it as the American one about the sea captain who punched a hole through the centre of the doughnuts so he could hang them on his ship's wheel.

Another popular New Year's Eve speciality is the *appelbeignet* or *appelflap*, an apple fritter. Well made, it is a slice of spiced apple, coated with a very thin batter and fried quickly to delicious crispness before the apple gets mushy. A manuscript cookery book from 1430 gives a recipe for *Frytourys* which seem almost identical.[52]

You will need a deep-fat fryer or large pan of oil heated to 175°C for this recipe. Don't use the metal basket – the doughnuts might stick to it. My recipe uses milk, but my husband swears by a mixture of beer and water.

Yield: about 20 doughnuts

500g strong white flour	*2 eggs, well beaten*
¾ tsp salt	*350–400 ml milk, warmed*
1 tbsp sugar	*100g currants*
2 ¼ tsp easyblend yeast	*100g raisins*
zest of ½ lemon	*1 tart apple, grated*

1 tsp very finely chopped candied bitter orange peel (optional)

In a large bowl mix the flour, salt, sugar, yeast and lemon zest together. Add the eggs and milk and beat well for several minutes. Mix in the fruit, cover with a damp cloth and leave to rise until doubled in size. Don't deflate the batter once it has risen. To fry, dip two dessert spoons in oil or water and use them to lift a plum-sized portion of batter. Slide this gently into the hot oil. Don't fry too many at a time or they will be heavy and oily. Drain on absorbent paper. Serve warm, dusted with icing sugar.

BIBLIOGRAPHY

Aalbregtse, M.A., *Kezanse Kost*. Oostburg: Uitgeverij W.J. Pieters, 1967.

Assire, Jérôme, *The Book of Bread*. Paris: Flammarion, 1996.

Ayto, John, *The Diner's Dictionary. Food and Drink from A to Z*. Oxford: Oxford University Press, 1993.

Barneveld, D., *De Oude Banketbakkerij*. Bussum: C.A.J. van Dishoeck, 1968.

Betje de Goedkoope Keukenmeid, sixteenth facsimile ed. (1975). Den Haag: G.B. van Goor Zonen, 1850.

Bieleman, J., *Geschiedenis van de Landbouw in Nederland 1500–1950: Veranderingen en Verscheidenheid*. Meppel: Boom, 1992.

Bijl, Wim van der, *Banketbakken,* Deel 1–5. Amsterdam: de Spieghel, 1993.

Billiet, Daniel et al., *Sint Nicolaas van A tot Z*. Eindhoven: Stichting Nationaal Sint Nicolaas Comité, 1997.

Brenk, Gerrit van den, *T 'Zaamenspraken Tusschen een Mevrouw, Banketbakker en Confiturier*. Amsterdam: wed. J. van Egmont, 1752.

Burema, Lambertus, *De Voeding in Nederland van de Middeleeuwen tot de Twintigste Eeuw*. Assen: 1953.

Calvé's Recepten voor de Bakkerij. Delft: Oliefabrieken Calvé, n.d., *ca*. 1935.

De Cierlijcke Voorsnijdinghe Aller Tafel Gerechten. Amersterdam: H. Sweerts, 1664.

The Cocoa Manual, Cacao de Zaan B.V., 1993.

Coe, Sophie D. and Michael D., *The True History of Chocolate*. London: Thames and Hudson, 1996.

Collen, Jacques, *Lekker Limburg: Historische recepten met hedendaagse ingrediënten*. Antwerp: CODA, 1994.

David, Elizabeth, *English Bread and Yeast Cookery*. London: Penguin, 1979.

Dijk, Janet van, 'De koekjeswereld wankelt' in *NRC Handelsblad* 29/1/97.

Dorp-Kampers, H.E.V., *Mevr. H.E.V. Dorp-Kampers' Geïllustreerd Kookboek*. Amsterdam: L.J. van Veen, n.d. (early twentieth century).

Drijver, F.W., *Folklore*. Amsterdam: N.V. Amsterdamsche Boek en Courantmaatschappij, n.d.

'Dulcinearius', 'De Kermiskoek en de Liefde' in *Bakkerswereld*.

——, 'Het verleden van de Deventer koek' in *Bakkerswereld*.

Elderman, A., *Zo in de Praktijk*. Doetinchem: Missett, 1989.

Engels-Geurts, Wil and Netty, *Limburgs Vlaaienboek*. Weert: Uitgeverij M & P, 1989.

——, *Traditionele Feestgerechten het Jaar Door*. Weert: Uitgeverij M & P, 1988.

Efdée, Ria, *Beschuit, een Tere Juffer*. Den Haag: Verbisko, 1990.

De Ervárene en Verstandige Hollandsche Huyshoudster. Amsterdam: B. Mourik, 1720

Forbes, W.A., *De Oudhollandse Keuken*. Bussum: Uitgeversmaatschappij C.A.J. van Dishoeck, n.d.

Gilst, A.P., *Het Paasfeest in Geschiedenis en Volksgebruiken*. Enschede: Van de Berg, 1992.

Gouw, Jan ter, *De Volksvermaken*, reprint of 1870s original. Amsterdam: Vrienden van het Amsterdam-boek, n.d.

Graft, C.C. van de, *Nederlandse Volksgebruiken bij Hoogtijdagen* (rev. T.W.R. de Haan). Utrecht: Spectrum, 1978.

Griever, G., *Vaktheorie voor Banketbakkers*. 's-Gravenhage: N.V. Uitgeverij Nijgh & van Ditmar, n.d., *ca.* 1954.

Groot en Klein Banket voor de Banketbakkerij, door een Chef-Pâtissier, 4th ed. Deventer: N.V. Uitgeversmaatschappij A.E. Kluwer, 1946.

Haezebroek, Maria, *De Hedendaagsche Kookkunst,* facsimile edition of an 1890 household book. Gouda: G.B. van Goor Zonen, n.d.

Haitsma Mulier-van Beusekom, C.A.H. (ed.), *Winkler Prins Culinaire Encyclopedie*. Amsterdam/Brussels: Elsevier, 1957.

Houwink Hzn., R., *Koekplanken als Volkskunst*. Assen: van Gorcum & Co, n.d.

Huizinga, Johan, *Nederlands Beschaving in de Zeventiende Eeuw*. Amsterdam: Contact, 1998. (1st ed. 1941)

Jaine, Tom, *Making Bread at Home*. London: Weidenfeld & Nicolson, 1995.

Jansen-Sieben, Ria, and Johanna Maria van Winter, *De Keuken van de Late Middeleeuwen: een Kookboek uit de Lage Landen*. Amsterdam: Bert Bakker, 1989.

Jappe Alberts, W., C.N. Fehrmann and A.A. de Jonge, *Geïllustreerde Geschiedenis van Nederland* (3rd ed.). 's-Gravenhage: Kruseman's Uitgeversmaatschappij B.V., 1978.

Jobse-van Putten, Josien, *'N Brood is Ginnen Stoeten*. Amsterdam: PJ Meertens Instituut, 1980.

——, *De Krentenwegge*. Amsterdam: PJ Meertens Instituut, 1992.

——, *Eenvoudig maar Voedzaam; Cultuurgeschiedenis van de Dagelijkse Maaltijd in Nederland*. Nijmegen: SUN Memoria & PJ Meertens Instituut Amsterdam, 1996.

Kooning, H.W., *Receptenboek voor den Banketbakker,* Deel I, 3rd ed. Doetinchem: Uitgevers-Mij. C. Misset N.V., 1942.

Koster, M., *Vakbekwaamheid voor Brood- en Banketverkopers(sters) in Verband met de Vestigingseisen*. 's-Gravenhage: Stichting voor Vakopleiding en Examens in het Bakkersbedrijf, 1938.

Koster, M., G. Griever and D. van Heel, *Vademecum voor de Banketbakkerij,* Deel II. Amsterdam: Vereniging voor de Bevordering van Vakopleidingen in het Banketbakkersbedrijf, 1955.

Kruizinga, J.H., *Levende Folklore in Nederland en Vlaanderen.* Assen: De Torenlaan, n.d.

Kuyper, Ben J., *50 Streekgerechten.* Wageningen: Zomer en Keuning, 1968.

Laan, K. ter, *Van Goor's Folkloristisch Woordenboek van Nederland en Vlaams Belgie.* Den Haag: van Goor, 1974.

Lee-van der Heijden, Janny van der, *Pannekoeken, Poffertjes en Wafels.* Bussum: van Dishoeck, 1983.

——, *Van het Hollandse Land: Streekrecepten uit de Provincie.* Bussum: van Dishoeck, 1982.

Lotgering-Hillebrand, R., *Wij Bakken Zelf!* Amsterdam: van Holkema & Warendorf's Uitgevers-Mij, 1932.

——, *Ieder z'n Meug. Smulbiek van Nederlandsche Volksgerechten.* Baarn: Bosch en Keuning, 1935.

McGee, Harold, *On Food and Cooking.* London: HarperCollins, 1991.

Manden, A.C., *Recepten van de Haagsche Kookschool.* 's-Gravenhage: De Gebroeders van Kleef, 1899.

Mariani, John F., *The Dictionary of American Food and Drink.* New York: Hearst Books, 1994.

Menkveld, H. and R. van Til, *Waarin Bakt de Bakker,* 7th ed. Purmerend: J. Muusses, 1960.

Meulen, Hielke van der, *Traditionele Streekproducten: Gastronomisch Erfgoed van Nederland.* Doetinchem: Elsevier Bedrijfsinformatie, 1998.

Miller, Russel et al., *De Oostindiëvaarders.* Amsterdam: Time Life, 1981.

Molen, J.R. ter, *Brood: de Geschiedenis van het Brood en het Broodgebruik in Nederland.* Rotterdam: Museum Boymans van Beuningen, 1983.

Molen, S.J. van der, *Levend Volksleven.* Assen: 1961.

Moonen, Marianne en Riek van Rhijn, *Neerlands Dis.* Utrecht: Spectrum, 1983.

Nannings, J.H., *Brood- en Gebaksvormen en Hunne Beteekenis in de Folklore.* Scheveningen, 1932.

Nap, E.J. and B. Muller, *De Koekbakkerij.* Doetinchem: Uitgeversmij C. Misset N.V., n.d.

Nicolas, Edm., *Over Graan, Meel en Brood.* Zeist: Centraal Instituut voor Voedingsonderzoek TNO, n.d.

Nieuw Vaderlandsche Kookkunst, by Twee, in Dit Vak Zeer Ervarene Huishoudsters. Amsterdam: J. Allart, 1797.

De Nieuwe, Welervarene Utrechtsche Keuken-Meid, Confituur-maakster en Huis-dokteres. Utrecht: G. v.d. Brink, Jansz., 1769.

Een Notabel Boecxken van Cokeryen. First published in Brussels, *ca.* 1510 by Thomas Vander Noot, this edition edited and annotated by Ria Jansen-Sieben and Marleen van der Molen-Willebrands. Amerstam: Uitgeverij De KAN.

Nyland, P.C., *Den Ervaren Huys-houder, Zijnde het III Deel*. Amsterdam: M. Doornick, 1668.

Oirschot, A. van, *Plaatselijke en Gewestelijke Specialiteiten uit Nederland*. Helmond: Uitgeverij Helmond, 1974.

Otterloo, Anneke H. van, *Eten en Eetlust in Nederland 1840–1990*. Amsterdam: Bert Bakker, 1990.

Polak, B.E., *Recepten uit de Joodse Keuken*. Amsterdam: N.V. de Arbeiderspers, 1956.

Polak & Polak, *Recepten uit de Joodse Keuken* (new revised ed.). Amsterdam: B.V. Uitgeverij de Arbeiderspers, 1996.

Raap, J.W., *Holland en de Hollanders*. Hollandse Maatschappij van Land-bouw, n.d. (>1975).

Riley, Gillian, *The Dutch Table*. Rohnert Park, Ca.: Pomegranate Artbooks, 1994.

Roos, Jeanne, *Het Snoepers Leesboek*. Haarlem: Magazijn de Bijenkorf, 1991.

Rose, Peter G., *Foods of the Hudson*. Woodstock: Overlook Press, 1993.

Rosengarten, F., *Het Grote Boek der Specerijen*. Amsterdam: De Driehoek, 1976.

Rotte, P.G., 'Zuidlaarderbollen en Toondagkoeken' in *Bakkerswereld*.

Schama, Simon, *The Embarrassment of Riches. An Interpretation of Dutch Culture in the Golden Age*, New York 1987, Dutch translation: *Overvloed en Onbehagen. De Nederlandse Cultuur in de Gouden Eeuw*. Amsterdam: Contact, 1988.

Schoep, C.J. and J. van der Lee, *Inleiding tot de Theorie van het Bakkersvak*, Deel II Het Rijs- en Bakproces. Deventer: Uitgeversmij. A.E. Kluwer, 1942.

Schilstra, J.J., *Koekplanken*. Bussum: Uitgeversmaatschappij C.A.J van Dishoeck, 1961.

Stoll, F.M. and W.H. de Groot, *Recepten Huishoudschool Laan van Meer-dervoort 's-Gravenhage*, nineteenth revised edition. 's-Gravenhage: de Gebroeders van Kleef, 1950.

Sultan, William, *Practical Baking*, 5th ed. New York: van Nostrand Reinhold, 1990.

'Techniek Verdringt Traditie', article in *de Telegraaf* 24/12/1928.

Toussaint-Samat, Maguelonne, *A History of Food*. Oxford: Blackwell, 1992.

Van Dale, *Groot Woordenboek der Nederlandse Taal* (3 vols.), 12th ed. Utrecht/ Antwerp: Van Dale Lexicografie, 1992.

Van Dale, *Groot Woordenboek Nederlands-Engels*, 2nd ed. Utrecht/ Antwerp: Van Dale Lexicografie, 1991.

Vandommele, Herman, *Appelen voor Miljoenen: de Geschiedenis van Paradijsappel tot Golden Delicious*. Privately published St Niklaas, 1980.

Veer, Annie van 't, *Oud-Hollands Kookboek*. Utrecht: Spectrum, 1966.

Ven, D.J. van de, Archives containing published and unpublished articles, drafts and essays.

——, *Als de Oogst Wordt Ingehaald*. Baarn: Bosch en Keuning, n.d. (>1931).

——, *Feestbrood in Midwintertijd*. Baarn: Bosch en Keuning, n.d. (>1923).

——, *Neerlands Volksleven*. Zaltbommel: N.V. Uitgeversmaatschappij en Boekhandel v/h P.M. Wink, 1920.

——, *Ons Eigen Volk in het Feestelijke Jaar*. Ca. 1942.

——, *Van Driekoningen en Keuninkje Spelen*. Baarn: Bosch en Keuning, n.d. (>1933).

——, *Van Nederlandsche Luilakken*. Baarn: Bosch en Keuning, n.d. (>1933).

Verhagen, G.H.M.J., *Rationeele Broodvoorziening in Nederland*. Leiden: N.V. Boek- en Steendrukkerij Eduard Ijdo, n.d., *ca.* 1942.

De Verstandige Huys-houdster, Voor-schrijvende de Alderwijste Wetten om Profijtelick, Gemackelick en Vermakelick te Leven, so in de Stadt als op 't Lant. Amsterdam: Cornelis Janszoon, 1661.

De Volmaakte Geldersche Keuken-Meyd. Nijmegen: Isaac van Campen, 1768.

De Volmaakte Hollandsche Keukenmeid. Amsterdam: S. van Esveldt, 1767.

Voskuil, J.J. et al., *Twaalf Bakkers en Twee Bakkersdochters*. Wageningen/ Arnhem: Genootschap voor de Bakkerij/Het Nederlands Openlucht Museum, 1978.

Voskuil, J.J. 'De Weg naar Luilekkerland' in *Bijdragen en Mededelingen Betreffende de Geschiedenis der Nederlanden*. Ned. Historisch Genootschap Dl. 98 Afl. 3, 1983.

Wasmus, Jan et al., *Het Sint Nicolaas Feestboek*. Amsterdam: De Bijenkorf, 1993.

Winter, Johanna Maria van, *Van Soeter Cokene: Recepten uit de Romeinse en Middeleeuwse Keuken*. Bussum: Unieboek/Grolsch/Spieghel Historiael, 1976.

Wolbert, Leo, *Praktijk Banketbakken*, Deel I en II. Helmond: Uitgeverij Helmond, 1983.

Zierikhoven, Catharina van (pseudonym of J.A. de Chalmot), *Volkoomen Nederlansch Kookkundig Woordenboek*. Leeuwaarden: H.A. de Chalmot, 1772.

Notes and References

Chapter One: The Dutch Baker

1. See 'New Year's Eve Doughnuts' in the Seasonal Baking section.
2. Voskuil et al., p. 9.
3. Ibid., p. 53.
4. Ibid., p. 9.
5. ter Molen, p. 21.
6. Verhagen, p. 1.
7. Voskuil et al. In this book of 14 interviews, the country bakers recall almost to a man the hazards of producing a decent loaf from the dough brought in by customers.
8. ter Molen, p. 24.
9. Verhagen, p. 2.
10. ter Molen, p. 26.
11. Ibid., p. 27.
12. Ibid., p. 27.
13. Burema, p. 26.
14. Ibid., p. 143, eighteenth century.
15. ter Molen, p. 29.
16. Burema, p. 40.
17. Ibid., p. 26.
18. ter Molen, p. 26.
19. Ibid., p. 49.
20. Verhagen, Annex IX shows that in a few areas 1 cent more is charged per two brown or white loaves costing between 16 and 18 cents. There is apparently no extra charge for coarse rye bread, but closer inspection shows that the bakers who charge extra don't appear to make rye bread.
21. ter Molen, p. 17.
22. Ibid., p. 15.
23. Ibid., p. 9.
24. Bieleman, p. 85.
25. Ibid., p. 85.
26. Ibid., p. 90.
27. Ibid., p. 192.
28. ter Molen, p. 11.
29. Burema, p. 13.
30. Bieleman, p. 35.
31. Schama, p. 176.
32. ter Molen, p. 12.
33. Ibid.
34. Voskuil, p. 466.
35. ter Molen, p. 35.
36. Verhagen, p. 5.
37. Ibid., p. 6.

Chapter Two: Bread

1.	ter Molen, p. 64 and Burema, p. 72.
2.	Forbes, p. 9.
3.	ter Molen, p. 65.
4.	Burema, p. 89.
5.	Burema, p. 89.
6.	Burema, pp. 97–98.
7.	Burema, p. 106.
8.	Burema, p. 106.
9.	Jobse-van Putten 1996, p. 258.
10.	See Schama, p. 161.
11.	Burema, p. 36.
12.	Burema, p. 72.
13.	*De Verstandige Huys-houdster*, p. 16.
14.	Burema, p. 141.
15.	See for example Schama, p. 176 and ter Molen, pp. 61–62. These percentages represent the most and least favourable situation for a family of two adults and two children.
16.	Burema, p. 90.
17.	Burema, p. 222.
18.	Burema, p. 38.
19.	Voskuil (p. 472) considers the stigmatization of rye bread to date from the seventeenth century.
20.	ter Molen, p. 64.
21.	ter Molen, p. 61.
22.	Burema, p. 73.
23.	Burema, p. 78.
24.	Voskuil, p. 461 and, p. 479.
25.	Burema, p. 140.
26.	ter Molen, p. 63.
27.	Voskuil, p. 479.
28.	Voskuil, p. 469.
29.	See Voskuil, p. 474–475.
30.	ter Molen, p. 62.
31.	Forbes, p. 60.
32.	Burema, p. 140.
33.	See van der Ven 'Als de Oogst wordt ingehaald', pp. 26–27.
34.	Burema, p. 221 mentions it being served by prosperous Frisian farmers around the mid nineteenth century.
35.	Voskuil et al., p. 117.
36.	ter Molen, p. 75.
37.	ter Molen, p. 80.
38.	van de Graft, pp. 102–103.
39.	van der Ven 1920.
40.	Nannings, p. 96.
41.	See articles, 'Merkwaardige brooduitdelingen en broodspinden in Nederland', p. 676.
42.	Theo Spil, baker and owner of the bakery museum in Medemblik, which

is not far from Wieringen, tells me that the custom died out faily recently.

43. Nannings, p. 152.
44. de Joode, p. 69.
45. 'Albertus Magnus, de vertutibus herbarum, lapidum, animalum et mirabilibus mundi', see Burema, p. 37.
46. Burema pp 89–90.
47. See van 't Veer, pp. 93–100.
48. ter Molen, p. 62.
49. Burema, p. 27.
50. Voskuil, p. 471.
51. Haezebroek, p. 123.
52. Assire, p. 34.
53. David, p. 95.
54. ter Molen, p. 32.
55. See ter Molen, p. 27.
56. See for example Koster, pp. 22–23, and ter Molen, pp. 52–55.
57. Jobse-van Putten 1996, p. 309.
58. Burema, p. 73.
59. de Joode, p. 33.
60. Burema, p. 91.
61. See for example de Joode, p. 36. Nowadays the vast majority of butter sold is unsalted.
62. Jobse-van Putten 1996, p. 234.
63. Burema, p. 41.
64. Burema, p. 73.
65. Burema, p. 92.
66. Burema, p. 105.
67. de Joode, p. 34.
68. See for example Jobse-van Putten 1996, p. 314, and de Joode, p. 36.
69. Jobse-van Putten 1996, p. 157.
70. de Joode, p. 30.
71. Jobse-van Putte 1996, p. 100.
72. Burema, p. 104.
73. van 't Veer, p. 118.
74. Burema, p. 257.
75. Jobse-van Putten 1996, p. 313.
76. Voskuil, p. 467.
77. Voskuil et al., pp. 6 and 67 give examples.
78. ter Molen, p. 63.
79. Voskuil et al., p. 66.
80. Voskuil et al., p. 62.
81. ter Molen, p. 34.
82. Voskuil et al., p. 64.
83. Voskuil et al., p. 65.
84. ter Laan, p. 322.
85. ter Laan, p. 492.
86. Voskuil et al., p. 65.
87. Schoep and van der Lee, p. 98.

88. Schoep and van der Lee, p. 99.
89. Koster, p. 31.
90. Voskuil et al., p. 50.
91. Koster, p. 32.
92. Koster, p. 32.
93. Voskuil et al., p. 64.
94. Voskuil et al., p. 20.
95. Burema, p. 226.
96. Voskuil et al., p. 22.
97. Jobse-van Putten 1992, p. 39. Moonen and van Rhijn also give a recipe for a turban-shaped *boffert*, to be baked for a baptism, p. 79.
98. See van 't Veer, p. 139.
99. Burema, p. 97.
100. Jobse-van Putten 1996, p. 367.
101. Burema, p. 221.
102. See Aalbregtse, pp. 139–141 for further detail.
103. Betje, p. 119.
104. ter Molen, p. 54, note 18.
105. See Aalbregtse, p. 101.
106. Polak & Polak, p. 130.

Chapter Three: Rusks

1. ter Molen, p. 29.
2. Ibid., p. 29.
3. Efdée, p. 23.
4. See table in Burema, pp. 108–109.
5. ter Molen, p. 62.
6. Burema, p. 182.
7. Burema, p. 110. In 1671 the biscuit brought back to Hellevoetsluis was inspected and considered fit enough to be used on a voyage the following spring.
8. Burema, p. 90.
9. ter Molen, p. 30.
10. *De Verstandige Huys-houdster*, p. 18.
11. *De Ervárene en Verstandige Hollandsche Huyshoudster*, p. 134. Plagiarism of cookbooks being as rife as it was in those days, this leaves room for conjecture.
12. See for example van den Brenk (1752) p. 17 and *Nieuw Welervarene Utrechtse Keuken-Meid* (1769), p. 109 recipe no. 121.
13. See *Nieuwe Welervarene Utrechtse Keuken-Meid,* p. 109, recipe no. 122.
14. Efdée, p. 27.
15. Jansen-Sieben and van Winter, p. 51.
16. Johannes le Francq van Berkhey (1729–1812), as quoted in de Joode, p. 42.
17. van den Brenk, pp. 22–23 gives recipes for smooth *gezuikerde anys* (sugared aniseed) as well as rough *jongens muisjes* (boys' mice), so the name *muisjes* was already known at that time. Interestingly, he also gives a recipe for *gezuikerde erwten* (sugared peas) which turn out to be sugar-

coated coriander, no longer eaten in Holland, but still made in countries like Turkey.
18. Schoep and van der Lee, p. 102.
19. Ibid., p. 102.
20. *Calvé's Recepten* gives 3 recipes for rusk jelly using Marseille soap, p. 52.
21. On display at Bakery Museum 'de Oude Bakkerij' in Medemblik.
22. Nicolas, p. 45.

Chapter Four: Spice Cakes
1. Roos, p. 75, Dutch army issued in 1938 with brandname koek.
2. Jansen-Sieben and van Winter, p. 10.
3. Rosengarten, p. 43, from a German price table dated 1393.
4. Miller et al., p. 26.
5. Jappe Alberts et al., p. 130.
6. van 't Veer, p. 48. *Een Notabel Boecxken van Cokeryen* records a similar recipe (number 82), and recipe number 87 describes how to make spice cakes expressly for use in sauces.
7. Jansen-Sieben and van Winter, p. 136.
8. Burema, p. 33.
9. Dulcinearius, 'Het verleden van de Deventerkoek', pp. 106–107.
10. See for example Nannings, p. 161, and Dulcinearius, op. cit., p. 107.
11. Dulcinearius, op. cit., p. 106.
12. ter Gouw, p. 370.
13. ter Gouw, p. 387, description of skating in the seventeenth century.
14. Roos, p. 74.
15. Nap and Muller, p. 8.
16. Bieleman, p. 197.
17. Nap and Muller, p. 8.
18. Ibid., p. 11.
19. Ibid., pp. 5 and 15.
20. Voskuil et al., p. 139.
21. Nannings, p. 188. The pun in Dutch is on the word '*pil*' which can mean pill or something lozenge shaped or elongated, like the spice loaves in question.

Chapter Five: Cakes
1. *De Volmaakte Geldersche Keuken-meid* gives such recipes, e.g. pp 273-274; and see van Winter, p. 131.
2. Polak 1956, p. 71.
3. Polak & Polak, 1996.
4. Jansen-Sieben and van Winter, p. 110, *Borbonoestaerten in de vasten*.
5. See for example van 't Veer, p. 54 and van Winter, p. 79.
6. See *De Cierlijcke Voorsnijdinghe*, pp. 33 and 95.
7. Dominee Belcampius, as quoted by Schama, p. 174.
8. Jobse-van Putten, 1996, p. 114.
9. Manden, p. 28.
10. Kooning, pp. 165–173.

11. There were two Dutch pounds at the time, the *Amsterdamse* and *Haagse pond,* respectively 494.09g and 469.73g. An ounce *(ons)* was 30.88g. An *ons* in contemporary usage denotes 100g.
12. *De Nieuwe, Welervarene Utrechtsche Keuken-meid, Confituur-maakster en Huis-doctores*, p. 85, recipe no. 51.
13. *Een Notabel Boecxken van Cokeryen*, recipe number 123.
14. Jansen-Sieben and van Winter, p. 88.
15. van Winter, p. 131.
16. Jansen-Sieben and van Winter, p. 139.
17. Many of the older books I consulted often gave two methods of baking: one for an oven and the other for a *taartepan*
18. van 't Veer, p. 81.
19. Jansen-Sieben and van Winter, p. 89.
20. Vandommele, p. 119.
21. For more detail see for example *The Cocoa Manual*, p. 22, Coe, pp. 241–242 and Roos, pp. 33–34.
22. Roos, p. 34.
23. *Betje de Goedkoope Keukenmeid*, p. 110, *Chocoladetaart*.

Chapter Six: Flans

1. Collen, p. 161.
2. Roos, p. 125.
3. Engels-Geurts 1994, p. 9.
4. Gilst, p. 59.
5. Engels-Geurts 1994, p. 12.
6. *Een Notabel Boexcken van Cokeryen*, recipe number 122. This flan has no crust.
7. Eighty Year War, 1566–1648.
8. Aalbregtse, p. 72 suggests either. A mid-nineteenth-century recipe for 'Spaansche brij' (*Betje de Goedkope Keukenmeid*, p. 93) uses rose-water.
9. Jansen-Sieben and van Winter, p. 154.
10. Ibid., p. 88.
11. Een Notabel Boecxken van Cokeryen, recipe number 117.
12. Jansen-Sieben and van Winter, p. 107.
13. Ibid., p. 132, quoting from 'Het kookboec oft Familieren Keukenboec' by M. Antonius Magirus.

Chapter Seven: Biscuits

1. Mariani, p. 93 informs us that the word 'cookie' first appears in print in 1703.
2. Roos, p. 105.
3. For example van 't Veer, pp. 146–147.
4. Betje, p. 116.
5. Ibid., p. 120.
6. Ibid., pp. 121 and 123.
7. Nannings, p. 168.
8. Roos, p. 77.
9. Ibid., p. 49.

10. See for example van 't Veer, p. 153 and *Betje*, p. 120.
11. Jobse-van Putten 1996, p. 221.
12. Forbes, p. 53.
13. Betje, p. 111.
14. Jobse-van Putten 1996, p. 107.
15. Ibid., p. 213.
16. ter Gouw, p. 59.
17. See for example *abricosen koekjes* (apricot biscuits) Forbes, p. 51 and redcurrant and raspberry versions in van 't Veer, p. 129.
18. van 't Veer, p. 122.
19. Roos, p. 111.
20. Schama, p. 548.
21. Nannings, p. 226.
22. van 't Veer, p. 146.

Chapter Eight: Pancakes

1. For recipe examples see van 't Veer, p. 155 and *Betje*, p. 130.
2. See for example Manders, p. 208.
3. Ibid., p. 242.
4. van 't Veer, pp. 50–51.
5. Jansen-Sieben and van Winter, p. 144.
6. van 't Veer, p. 152.
7. ter Gouw, p. 201.
8. Burema, p. 141.
9. Burema, p. 141.
10. Jobse-van Putten 1996 observes this in several places.
11. Jobse-van Putten 1996, p. 439.
12. Haitsma Mulier-van Beusekom, p. 364.
13. Aalbregtse, p. 143–144.
14. Forbes, p. 85.
15. See for example Forbes, p. 86 and *Betje*, p. 113.
16. Lotgering-Hillebrand (*Ieder z'n Meug*), p. 11. *Betje* offers a recipe, p. 115.
17. *Betje*, pp. 154 and 155.
18. Icing sugar has been used on pancakes since the Middle Ages, finely ground loaf sugar, referred to as powdered sugar which is still the Dutch name.
19. Burema, p. 171.
20. Burema, p. 141.
21. Jobse-van Putten 1996, p. 285.
22. Haezebroek, p. 158.

Chapter Nine: Waffles and Wafers

1. van de Graft, p. 23.
2. ter Gouw, footnote on, p. 112.
3. See the relevant chapters in van de Graft and ter Gouw.
4. ter Gouw, pp. 171–185 conveys this impression.
5. van de Graft, p. 33.

6.   van der Ven, p. 17.
7.   Kruizinga, p. 40.
8.   See among others ter Gouw, p. 116 and ter Molen, p. 56.
9.   van der Ven, *Feestbrood in Midwintertijd*, p. 20.
10.   van der Ven op. cit., p. 15 shows an example.
11.   Ibid., p. 20.
12.   ter Gouw, pp. 109–110.
13.   van der Ven, *Feestbrood in Midwintertijd*, p. 12.
14.   van de Graft, pp. 24 and 26 and van der Ven, *Feestbrood in Midwintertijd*, pp. 12 and 16.
15.   Ibid., p. 20.
16.   van der Ven, p. 16.
17.   ter Laan, p. 259.
18.   van der Ven, p. 15.
19.   Jansen-Sieben and van Winter, pp. 94–95.
20.   See for example van 't Veer, pp. 148–150.
21.   This information is proffered on the website of the Gouda wafer industry: www.goudsewafelindustrie.nl.
22.   Jansen-Sieben and van Winter, p. 94.
23.   Aalbregtse, p. 136.
24.   van de Graft, p. 20.
25.   Aalbregtse, p. 146.

Chapter Ten: Seasonal Baking

1.   Nannings, pp. 115–116.
2.   ter Gouw, p. 206.
3.   At that time, there were two pound measures, the *Amsterdamse* and *Haagse pond:* 494.09g and 469.73g respectively.
4.   Op cit. p. 16, recipe no. 44.
5.   See for example Voskuil et al., p. 8 and Nannings, p. 122.
6.   'Techniek Verdringt Traditie', newspaper article in *de Telegraaf*, 24/12/1928.
7.   Voskuil et al., p. 117.
8.   Voskuil et al., p. 116.
9.   See for example van der Ven, *Van Driekoningenavond...*, pp. 38–43.
10.   Nannings, p. 149, one of a number of examples of verses.
11.   ter Laan, p. 190.
12.   Ibid.
13.   Ibid., p. 279.
14.   Nannings, p. 147.
15.   Ibid.
16.   P.G.Rotte, 'Zuidlaarderbollen en Toondagkoeken', article in *Bakkerswereld.*
17.   Dulcinearius, 'De Kermiskoek en de Liefde'.
18.   See recipe, van 't Veer, p. 144.
19.   See *Nieuw Vaderlandsche Kookkunst,* p. 320 and *Volmaakte Hollandsche Keuken-meid,* p. 12 n. 23, respectively.
20.   For detailed information see Jobse-van Putten, *De Krentenwegge* (1992),

an in-depth survey of this bread, its origins and implications.

21.   Jobse-van Putten (1992), p. 19.
22.   Ibid., p. 30.
23.   Kruizinga, p. 248.
24.   Moonen and van Rhijn, p. 96.
25.   Nannings, p. 109.
26.   See van der Graft, pp. 74ff. She is the recognized expert on this subject.
27.   Voskuil et al., p. 78.
28.   van der Graft, p. 70. An example from eastern Holland.
29.   Gilst, p. 12.
30.   Billiet et al., p. 17.
31.   Billiet et al., p. 20.
32.   Wasmus et al., p. 11.
33.   Billiet et al., p. 76.
34.   Wasmus et al., p. 56.
35.   Roos, p. 98.
36.   Billiet et al., p. 51.
37.   Ibid.
38.   Ibid.
39.   Roos, p. 87.
40.   van der Ven, *Feestbrood in Midwintertijd*, p. 24.
41.   Nannings, p. 56.
42.   Nannings gives several examples in chapters 6 and 7.
43.   ter Gouw, p. 168.
44.   See for example van der Ven, *Feestbrood in Midwintertijd*, p. 22 and Nannings, p. 57.
45.   Haitsma Mulier-van Beusekom, *Winkler Prins Culinaire Encyclopedie*.
46.   See ter Gouw, p. 659.
47.   *Betje*, p. 119.
48.   Mariani, p. 111.
49.   As quoted by Mariani, p. 111.
50.   The word 'cruller' undeniably stems from the Dutch word *krullen*, meaning 'to curl'.
51.   Taken from one of the several internet sites that offer 'The Legend of Sleepy Hollow'.
52.   See van Winter, p. 142.

Index of recipes, foreign words, personal and place names.